Frank Owen was born in 1905 and educated at Monmouth School and at Sidney Sussex College, Cambridge. He was Editor of both the *Evening Standard* (1938–41) and the *Daily Mail* (1947–50). During the Second World War he served in the Royal Armoured Corps from 1942 to 1943 and South-East Asia Command from 1944 to 1946. He was one of the very first British officers to re-enter Singapore when the War ended and was present at the official surrender of the Japanese on 12 September 1945. His books include *His was the Kingdom* (1937), an account of the abdication of Edward VIII; *Guilty Men* (with Michael Foot and Peter Howard, 1938); *The Three Dictators* (1940); *The Campaign in Burma* (1946); *Tempestuous Journey: Lloyd George, His Life and Times* (1954); *Peron: His Rise and Fall* (1957); and *The Fall of Singapore* (1960; Classic Penguin, 2001). He received an OBE and was a Freeman of the City of London. Frank Owen died in 1979.

The Last March, February 15, 1942. Lieut.-General A. E. Percival, G.O.C. Malaya (extreme right), and British officers bearing the Union Jack and the white flag of truce going to sign the deed of surrender at the headquarters of Lieut.-General Tomoyuki Yamashita at Bukit Timah village on Singapore Island

FRANK OWEN

The Fall of Singapore

PENGUIN BOOKS

PENGUIN BOOKS

Published by the Penguin Group
Penguin Books Ltd, 80 Strand, London, WC2R 0RL, England
Penguin Putnam Inc., 375 Hudson Street, New York, New York 10014, USA
Penguin Books Australia Ltd, 250 Camberwell Road, Camberwell, Victoria 3124, Australia
Penguin Books Canada Ltd, 10 Alcorn Avenue, Toronto, Ontario, Canada M4V 3B2
Penguin Books India (P) Ltd, 11 Community Centre, Panchsheel Park, New Delhi – 110 017, India
Penguin Books (NZ) Ltd, Cnr Rosedale and Airborne Roads, Albany, Auckland, New Zealand
Penguin Books (South Africa) (Pty) Ltd, 24 Sturdee Avenue, Rosebank 2196, South Africa

Penguin Books Ltd, Registered Offices: 80 Strand, London, WC2R 0RL, England

www.penguin.com

First published by Michael Joseph 1960
Published as a Classic Penguin 2001

1

Copyright © Beaverbrook Newspapers, 1960

CONTENTS

ILLUSTRATIONS

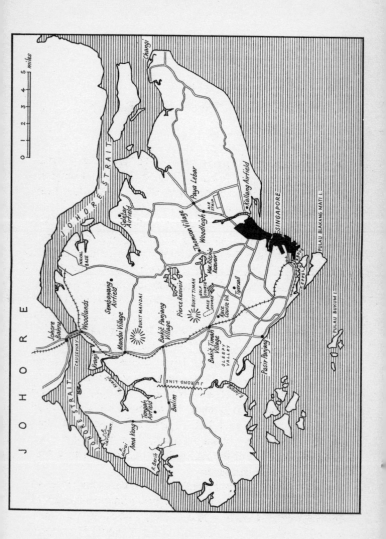

CHAPTER ONE

THE FLAG THEY NEVER LOST

A RADIO picture in the Second World War, widely repro-
duced in the newspapers of Great Britain, the Commonwealth and the United States of America, shocked opinion
throughout the English-speaking world.

It showed a squad of men, two of whom carried flags over
their shoulders, marching along a sunlit village street in the
Island of Singapore. The furthermost flag was a Union Jack,
the near one a white flag of truce. Their bearers were British
officers, in shorts, shirts and steel helmets, and by their side
stamped high-booted Japanese armed escorts. Included in the
party was Lieut. General Percival[1], commanding the troops
who were the last British garrison of Fortress Singapore. He
had come to sign the deed of its surrender.

The fall of Singapore, so long believed (and so often
boasted) by British leaders to be an 'impregnable citadel,'
a 'bastion of Empire,' the 'Gibraltar of the Far East', and
the loss of the great modern Naval Base on which some
£63,000,000 or so had been spent before the war, had
already on the day of capitulation, 15th February 1942,
stunned the public of the Allied countries, their Armed Services and their Governments.

For it seemed utterly incredible that a defending force of
85,000 men could have laid down their arms to invaders of
less numerical strength without even a show of resistance
in the streets of the greatest city in South-East Asia.

[1]Lieut. General A. E. Percival, C.B., D.S.O., O.B.E., M.C.

Now, more than a month later (17th March 1942) this shaming photographic record of the hour of Britain's deepest humiliation was flashed across the world.

Lieut. General Tomoyuki Yamashita, the conqueror of Singapore, had insisted on making the ceremony of surrender as degrading to his captives as Japanese arrogance and ingenuity could devise.

On the morning of that Black Sunday, 15th February 1942, Lieut. General Percival held a fateful conference at Fort Canning with his Senior Commanders. Both the continued defence of the city and the project of a last desperate counter-attack were debated, and rejected as impracticable. It was decided to send off a Joint Military and Civil deputation to the enemy lines to invite Japanese envoys to visit Singapore and discuss a cessation of hostilities.

They returned with orders that Percival himself must proceed with Staff Officers, bearing a Union Jack and a white flag of truce, to the Ford Automobile Works beyond Bukit Timah village, northward of Singapore City, where the Japanese Commander would lay down the terms of surrender. A further requirement was that the Japanese Rising Sun flag should be hoisted over the Cathay Building, the tallest in Singapore, so that the British troops should know that due submission had been made.

The final parley (if this one-sided dictation can be so described) took place towards evening of that sultry day. On the floor of the large Assembly Room in the Ford factory had been chalked the names of the many Japanese officers who were to be privileged to witness this official mortification of the beaten White Imperialists. They queued up, filed in, and took their seats on the floor. The four British envoys were then led to the table where General Yamashita sat with his Staff. He acknowledged them briefly, then read out from a paper before him the terms—or rather, the orders—of surrender. 'There was not much chance of bargaining' says Percival, but he claims, justly, that he did the best he could to ensure the safety of both troops and civilians.[1]

There was only one copy of the surrender document, and this, says Percival[2], the Japanese kept.

'Certainly no copy was handed to me. The actual terms of surrender cannot therefore be recorded accurately.'

But, as far as Percival's memory goes, he says[3] they included:

(1) The unconditional surrender of all military forces (Army, Navy and Air Force) in Singapore Area.

(2) Hostilities to cease at 8.30 p.m. that evening.

(3) All troops to remain in position until further orders.

(4) All weapons, military equipment, ships, planes and secret documents to be handed over intact.

(5) To prevent looting, etc., during the temporary withdrawal of all armed forces in Singapore, a force of 100 British armed men to take over until relieved by the Japanese.

Percival had already, earlier that day, issued orders to destroy before 4 p.m. all secret and technical equipment, ciphers, codes, secret documents and heavy guns[4]. Now, at Bukit Timah, he informed Yamashita of this, adding that no ships or planes remained in Singapore. The Japanese Commander accepted it. Hostilities ended that night.

According to Tokyo's *Domei News Agency*, Yamashita also accepted

'full responsibility for the lives of the British and Australian troops, as well as the British women and children remaining in Singapore. He declared "Rely on Japanese *Bushido*." *Bushido* is the ancient Japanese code of chivalry, inculcating courage, loyalty, courtesy and self-control.'

[1] In his book '*The War in Malaya*,' Lieut. General A. E. Percival, C.B., D.S.O., O.B.E., M.C. (Eyre & Spottiswoode).

[2] In his *Despatches*. London Gazette, 20th February 1948.

[3] See *Despatches*. *Ibid*.

[4] These orders, as we shall see, were not effectively carried out.

Although next morning, 16th February, the Japanese advance guards occupied the suburbs of Singapore, and a token 'Triumph Parade' of 175 Japanese medium and light tanks was staged through the main streets while Rising Sun flags fluttered in the breeze from all public buildings, the mass forces of the invading army never did enter the city. The teeming population of more than a million mixed peoples, Chinese, Indian, Malayan, British and Australian, were spared the horrors of the rape, murder and massacre which had disgraced the Japanese capture of Hong Kong the previous Christmas Day—and which had been among the reasons impelling General Percival to surrender Singapore and avoid a repetition of such lurid events here.

But *Bushido* soon ran out when it came to the treatment of the military prisoners-of-war.

Now, of the 85,000 troops who had passed under enemy rule by this surrender, some 45,000 were Indian. Two days after the fall of Singapore the Japanese imposed a colour bar, segregating all Indian ranks from their British and Australian comrades and putting them into a special camp at Farrar Park.

Here, they were exhorted by Indian deserters to enlist in the new 'Indian National Army' of Subhas Chandra Bose[1] which the Japanese were sponsoring for the invasion and 'Liberation' of India, next step in their own Greater East Asia plan of conquest.

Dazed and disillusioned by the disaster of Singapore and the apparent end of the British Raj, many of the younger Indian soldiers succumbed (and many were very young and, indeed, had far from completed their training as soldiers before being thrown into battle). But thousands of others refused to break their oath of loyalty, though cut off from their comrades and under the threat—and sometimes, actual

[1]Educated at Cambridge, Subhas Chandra Bose became a violent Indian Nationalist leader, was arrested by the British early in the war, released, made his way first to Berlin and then to Japanese-occupied Malaya. He was killed in an aeroplane crash August 1945.
The 'Indian National Army' eventually recruited as many as 25,000 ex-prisoners-of-war and deserters.

flail—of Japanese torture. The Gurkhas held out to a man.

As for the British and Australian prisoners-of-war, they were marched off to Changi Barracks, at the eastern end of Singapore Island, where they were herded into overcrowded prison pens. (They were even worse accommodated at the River Valley Camp, to which working parties were sent.) Prisoners who tried to escape and were re-captured were shot publicly. Many hundreds died from their wounds, from malaria, dysentery, beri-beri and other diseases. Thousands more would perish from sickness, exhaustion or savage ill-treatment on the 'Railway of Death,' which the Japanese built as a military supply line from Siam to Burma with forced labour drawn from their prison camps. Under the 'Code of Chivalry' called *Bushido* the casualty rate was far higher in the Japanese jails than on the battlefield.

Was it inevitable that so many soldiers who served under the Union Jack should have had to follow that flag into captivity in Singapore? That they should have had to spend, either the remainder of their life or the next three-and-a-half years of it, in a Japanese hell? Could not 'Fortress Singapore' have been held, as Winston Churchill himself believed it could almost up to the very day it fell?

There was some suggestion during the war that a Royal Commission should hold inquiry into the mystery of this 'impregnable citadel.' But Churchill, as Prime Minister, judged that this was not then possible. We could not spare the time, the men, or the energy while the war still raged in Europe, Africa, Burma and Indonesia. Parliament agreed with him.

Six years after the war was all over (1951), Churchill was writing[1]

'but I certainly thought that in justice to the officers and men concerned there should be an inquiry into all the circumstances as soon as the fighting stopped. This, how-

[1] In *The Second World War*. Vol. III. 'The Hinge of Fate' by Winston S. Churchill.

ever, has not been instituted by the Government of
the day.'

The British Government of that day (1951) was a Labour
one. Now, nine more years have gone by (including four
under a Churchill Tory Government and five more under
other Tory Governments), but no Royal Commission has
ever yet been set up to sift the mystery of the Fall of Singapore, and may be it is now too late, since many of the leading personalities have passed on.

True, there were published within a few years, the
Despatches of five British Commanding Officers (or Acting
C.O.'s), the personal narratives of two of the leading Service
figures, many references in their volumes by three historians
of the latest World War, and a score of interesting books by
fighting men, reporters and others who were actually on the
scene. But not until 1957 did any official British account
appear and even this disclaimed any attempt 'to be a
comprehensive history of the war against Japan.'[1]

Meantime, History itself had played its own strange tricks.

On another Sunday, 2nd September 1945, General Percival,
lately released from the Japanese jail in Manchuria to which
he had been transferred later in the war, was present in
Tokyo Bay when Japan formally surrendered to the victorious
Allies.

The Wheel of Fate completed its full turn next day when at
Manila, in the Philippine Islands, General Percival stood
alongside the United States Commander who had been
forced to surrender that great American base a few weeks
after the fall of Singapore. Signing the deed of capitulation
now for the beaten enemy, was General Tomoyuki Yamashita.
An eyebrow lifted, a flash of recognition—and then the
sphinx-like mask again of all the Sons of Nippon.

---

[1]See introduction to '*The War Against Japan.*' Vol I. by Major-General S.
Woodburn Kirby, C.B., C.M.G., C.I.E., O.B.E., M.C. (H.M. Stationery
Office).
    The Japanese Thrust, by Lionel Wigmore, an account, 'with full access to
official documents' was issued in the same year, 1957, by the Australian War
Memorial. (The Griffin Press, Adelaide.)

Later, Yamashita was set on trial for the crimes against humanity committed by his troops. He was executed.

There was a curious destiny, too, for that Union Jack which had been borne alongside the white flag of surrender through the Japanese lines beyond Singapore.

A few days later, the Japanese Commander demanded this Union Jack from the British officer concerned (by then, a prisoner-of-war in Changi Jail).

'You can't have it,' said the officer, 'it doesn't exist. I burned it that same night on the ramparts of Fort Canning, looking towards England and home.'

The Japanese took his word. In truth, the flag lay hidden in the jail. It was used many a time in the next three-and-a-half years for the funerals of British and Australian soldiers who died in captivity there, its story being unsuspected by the Japanese.

On the day that Singapore was formally liberated by the Allied Forces of South-East Asia Command, 12th September 1945, the Union Jack of the Men of Changi Jail was raised over the city that their comrades had redeemed.

But—*why did Singapore fall?*

CHAPTER TWO

RED LIGHT—IGNORED

SURELY, we had ample warning of what was coming to us?

The invasion of Malaya had been debated in high Japanese Council, decided, planned—and the seaborne landings and jungle operations for it militarily rehearsed by them for a dozen years before it happened. *And all the time the evidence was in our hands!*

First, there was certain unique historical documentation of their intent. That is, the detailed programme of Japan's Supreme Plan for the conquest of all East Asia—which was carried forward with time-table exactitude throughout the 'thirties.'

Next, with the advent of the Second World War (though long before Japan herself became engaged in December 1941), there piled up further proof that she was making ready to strike against us. This was shown, both by Japanese propaganda and political action, which firmly underlined the reports that steadily streamed in to us from secret sources in Tokyo, Shanghai, Chungking, Bangkok, Saigon and elsewhere. Thus, by mid-1940, we knew that the Japs planned to build 16 more capital warships.

Then, at the end of that year, the U.S. Intelligence Service pierced the Japanese cipher code and still more detailed and 'inside' information became available to us. For example, there was that message of 31st July 1941, from the Japanese

Foreign Minister to their Ambassador in Berlin, telling him to explain to Hitler why Japan was moving south instead of westward against Russia. Stressing the increasingly strained trade relations between Japan and the Anglo-American world, he said that his country 'must take immediate steps to break asunder the ever-strengthening chain of encirclement which is being woven under the guidance of and with the participation of England and the United States, acting like a cunning dragon seemingly asleep.'

We also knew from our own Secret Service that for years past the Japanese had been building up an elaborate network of agents in South-East Asia, where almost every other barber or photographer seemed to be a Jap. The Johore coast line opposite the Naval Base was riddled with their spies. They were left in peace to get on with their job because, since our substantial Intelligence organisation in Singapore, the Far Eastern Combined Bureau (F.E.C.B.), were able to intercept and decode their messages, the information they exchanged was reckoned well worthwhile to us. When the war broke out, however, we failed to locate those agents and round them up.

Final evidence of Japanese purpose was that for several days before Japanese bombers and landing-craft actually went into action over the towns and on the shores of Malaya, we had been aware of the obviously hostile movement of foreign cruisers, convoys and aircraft in the neighbouring seas.

When the first Japanese assault troops waded ashore that December midnight in North Malaya, and then the first Japanese bombs crashed down on Singapore City, it seems that the enemy reaped almost all the advantages of surprise.

WHY? After all these years, this angry question is still asked.

Let us examine, first, this written evidence, the blueprint of invasion. We do not here refer to the design of the Japanese Emperor Meiji and his Elder Statesmen, concerted half-a-

century earlier (and also steadily worked out subsequently[1]),
but to the notorious 'Tanaka Memorial' of 1929, which
brought up-to-date the plan for the Yamata Race (the
Japanese) to overrun half the earth within the next genera-
tion.

Baron Tanaka, a general of the Imperial Japanese Army
and Leader of the Seiyukai (Liberal) Party, was Prime
Minister of Japan, 1927-1929. In July of this last year, he
handed to the Emperor his own dynamic scheme of international plunder.

It urged the desperate need to solve Japan's problem of
how to provide living space for her ever-growing family, that
'surplus population' of 700,000 new bodies annually. Also,
how to secure the sources of her food supply and the raw
materials needed for her industry.

The Tanaka Memorial, this Nippon Leader's own *Mein
Kampf*, went on to lay down the order of acquisition of the
required loot. It ran this way:

**Grab China first! Then South-East Asia! Then India! Then
Australasia! Then the Middle East! Then Europe—and finally,
maybe the rest of the world[2].**

The Tanaka Memorial leaked out to the world the same
year that it was drafted. The Japanese Government promptly
and officially branded it as a forgery. Some mystery certainly
attended its original publication. A copy was reported to have

---

[1]By this policy, in 1894, Japan had attacked China and seized from her the
Island of Formosa, southward. Then, in 1904, at the time of the Russo-
Japanese War, she grabbed the island of Sakhalin, northward. She also planted
herself firmly on the Asian shore, at Port Arthur. Five years later, she annexed
Korea. Five more (at the outbreak of the First World War), and the German
concessions at Kiaochow and Tsingtao had passed into the Japanese bag. At
the Versailles Peace Treaty, 1919, the Japanese picked up mandates over the
ex-German colonies in the Marshall and the Caroline Isles of the Pacific Ocean.

[2]Thus: "In order to conquer China, we must first conquer Manchuria and
Mongolia. In order to win real rights in Manchuria and Mongolia, we must
first use this district as a base, then penetrate into the rest of China under the
pretext of developing our trade. Armed with already safeguarded rights, we
shall seize the entire land. If we are able to conquer China, all the other
Asiatic countries and the countries of the South Seas will fear us and will
capitulate before us. The world will then understand that East Asia is ours,
and will not dare to violate our rights. With all the resources of China at our
disposal, we shall press forward to the conquest of India, the Archipelago,
Asia Minor, Central Asia and even Europe.'

reached Shanghai during the autumn of 1929, where a version of it was printed in Chinese. Later, *The China Critic*, a local periodical, got hold of it and published an English translation, which was widely circulated, both in Britain and in the U.S.A.

Leon Trotsky, the Bolshevik leader whom Joseph Stalin ousted from power in Russia after the death of Lenin, expelled, and finally caused to be murdered in Mexico, revealed from exile that the pages of the Tanaka Memorial had been photographed by an employee in the Japanese Ministry of Naval Affairs at Tokyo, sold to a Russian agent for $3000, and that copies of the developed film had been sent by various routes to Moscow. The text was then duly passed on to various countries by roundabout means, because the Russian Government did not want to leave any clues as to their informants.

Whatever the explanation be as to the origin of the Tanaka Memorial, events certainly followed it with quite extraordinary precision.

In 1931, the Japanese seized Manchuria, defying the plaintive protests of the League of Nations, and setting up there a puppet State known as 'Manchukuo.' A year or two later, they had shoved into North China; and in 1937, protesting against 'Red lawlessness' in China and the attacks upon the property of Japanese traders there (the so-called 'China Incident'), they invaded the Eastern Provinces and established another Government of stooges at Nanking.

Looking back now, it seems incredible that no Government of any of the most closely interested countries, Britain, U.S.A., France and Holland, should have made any effort at that time (looking forward!) to arrange a joint guarantee of Indo-China, Siam, Malaya and Indonesia against Japanese aggression. It might well have kept Japan out of the Second World War, for if established it must have brought about some real co-operation, of which there turned out to be almost none until after battle had been joined.

Meantime, Japan's economic problems were piling up. In

the 'thirties, her industrial output doubled (largely in engineering and metals), which made her ever more desperately short of oil. For 80% of this supply, Japan relied on the United States, and for another 10% of it on the Dutch East Indies. And, incidentally, over the same period, Japan's military and naval expenditures rose from just under 30% of her National Budget to more than 70%.

Came the opening of that World War II—and with it, further signs of Japan's real purpose.

When this event occurred, the Japanese at first behaved very discreetly. They had taken rather anxious note of the Berlin-Moscow Pact of Non-Aggression, signed on 23rd August 1939 (which was the immediate prelude to the war). *Had Germany gained a free hand to deal with Europe in return for Russia getting a similar licence to settle accounts with Japan?* Tokio walked warily during those months of the 'phoney war' in Europe.

But after Dunkirk and the beginning of the bombing of Britain, the Japanese plainly showed that they were back on their old track again. Their Press and radio boomed propaganda about the 'Greater East Asia Co-Prosperity Sphere' (i.e. an expanding and dominating Empire of Japan). In September 1940, with Germany putting the squeeze on to the Vichy Government of France to offer no resistance, Japanese troops marched into the northern part of the French colony of Indo-China, giving them a fresh springboard to the South. That same month, a Tripartite Pact between Germany, Italy and Japan was signed, binding Japan to enter the war on the side of the Axis if the U.S.A. should join the Allies. This was intended to deter the Americans from Aid to Britain.

Meantime, German aircraft technicians were flying into Japan by hundreds, and a special Japanese Military Mission was off to Berlin. It was headed by Lieut. General Tomoyuki Yamashita, the soldier destined to command the invasion of Malaya and Singapore.

By New Year 1941, Japanese warships were reported to be anchored in French Indo-China's great port of Saigon, and also to be cruising in the Gulf of Siam. We know now, by the confession of von Ribbentrop at the Nuremberg Trial, that the Germans were continuously pressing the Japanese to attack Singapore right then.[1]

One leading figure in Britain seems to have had some appreciation of the danger in the Far East—or, at any rate, some flashes of it. Wrote the Prime Minister, Winston Churchill, to President Roosevelt on 8th December 1940:

> 'Japan is thrusting southward through Indo-China to Saigon and other naval and air bases, thus bringing them within a comparatively short distance of Singapore and the Dutch East Indies.'

[1] See *Nuremberg Documents* Part I.

And again to Roosevelt on 15th February 1941:

> 'Many drifting straws seem to indicate Japanese inten-
> tion to make war on us, or do something that would
> force us to make war on them in the next few weeks or
> months.'[1]

We write of Churchill's 'flashes' of understanding on the
problem threat in the Far East, because, frankly, that light
was intermittent.

Thus, on 13th February 1941 (i.e. between the two dates of
the above-quoted letters to Roosevelt), he dictated a minute
to the Chiefs of Staff, who were meeting to discuss plans to
send reinforcements to Singapore:

> 'I do not remember to have given my approval to these
> very large diversions of force. On the contrary, if my
> minutes are collected they will be seen to have had an
> opposite tendency. The political situation in the Far East
> does not seem to require, and the strength of our Air
> Force by no means warrants, the maintenance of such
> large forces in the Far East at this time.'[2]

Even as late as October 1941, it appears that Churchill was
doubtful of a Japanese attack in force on Malaya, believing
that the main danger would lie in their raids on the trade
routes by their new fast battleships.[3] In these circumstances
it is not surprising that subordinates in Government Departments took no energetic action to meet the threat in time.
The issue, of course, had been complicated by the sudden
German invasion of Russia in June 1941. The question then
arose (and had to be battled out in the highest quarters) as
to whether or not Britain could fight a major war both in the
West and in the East. It was decided against any powerful
reinforcement of the East. There remains the doubt if the little
that was done was well done.

[1] See *The Second World War*. Vol. II. By Winston S. Churchill. (Cassell &
Co Ltd.)
[2] See *The War Against Japan*. Vol. I (H.M. Stationery Office).
[3] *ibid.*

Meanwhile, in Japan, the 'War Now!' Movement was mounting in power.

For years past, there had been a serious division of opinion in that country, even between the Armed Services, as to Japan's prospects if she should get mixed up in a really big war again.

Thus, the Army Chiefs were always ready to take the risks involved in making a substantial landgrab in East Asia. But the Navy view, steadfastly expressed by Admiral of the Fleet Nagano, Chief of Naval Staff, was that Japan could not stand up to more than two years of war—even with the early loot quickly collected. The reason? Japan's dire lack of the raw materials and of the industrial/scientific machinery required to wage a modern war and still satisfy her own domestic needs. It was in pursuance of this anti-war line that in 1941, Admiral Nagano persuaded his colleague and friend, Admiral Kichisaburo Nomura, to accept the appointment of Japanese Ambassador to the United States.

But though this Navy 'peace policy' was still being urged, both at Japanese Imperial Headquarters and in the Cabinet Council as late as the autumn of that year, already ever since the early spring, Admiral Yamamoto, Commander-in-Chief of the Combined Fleet, had been working out a detailed strategic plan for a surprise attack on the U.S. naval base at Pearl Harbour in the Hawaiian Isles *the very moment that war became inevitable.*

As the months passed, that moment seemed to be drawing nearer. Not only the newspapers and the strongest political parties, but top-ranking public officials were clamantly demanding action. Thus, Toshio Shiratori, former Ambassador to Italy, and currently holding a vitally important Foreign Office post in Tokyo, declared that

> 'the war has now moved from China to South-East Asia, and is about to enter the stage of war for all Asia.'

The war had certainly moved South—and towards Singapore.

One of Japan's craftiest strokes had been to stir up trouble between the Government of Siam and the Vichy French Government, who still nominally ruled Indo-China. Siam claimed back certain provinces which had once been her's before being incorporated in the French colony. Having started a frontier *fracas* between the two, Japan, in her self-imposed role of mediator, insisted on her right to station troops, planes and warships at strategic points in Indo-China 'to preserve order.' (This police action, incidentally, coincided with an especially venomous and violent outburst in the Japanese Press against the 'foreign devils,' Britain and the U.S.A. in particular, who were seeking to 'sow hatred in the hearts of the people of these peace-loving lands').

After a token opposition, the feeble Vichy French Government yielded, 21st July 1941[1]. Within two or three days Japanese warships had taken over the naval base at Camranh Bay and a Japanese convoy had arrived at Saigon Harbour, 200 miles South-westward (in direct line to Malaya) and had disembarked an Occupation Force.

Officially, Tokyo gave it out that the Japanese military strength in Indo-China now amounted to 50,000. British Intelligence sources reckoned it at nearer 200,000—and they were shock troops, not reservists or trainees. By the end of the month, they were fully established and had begun building new airfields to the South and West. Japan had now got a naval base within 700 miles of Singapore, and an air base within 600 miles.

The American and British Governments acted firmly (though whether effectively is another matter). President Roosevelt at once required the Japanese Government to withdraw their troops, failing which he would freeze all Japanese

---

[1]In the summer of 1940, there had been some hope that Admiral Découx, the French Naval Commander, might accept the invitation to sail his ships to Singapore and join forces with the Free French remnant in the Far East. But then, the Vichy Government offered him the Governor-Generalship of Indo-China, which he accepted.

It appears that Découx remained deeply suspicious of Japan's designs, for he was still negotiating with the British authorities in Singapore during the spring of 1941. But it all ended up in talk.

trading assets in the United States. Great Britain took the
same course, and the Government of the Dutch East Indies
followed within a day or two. Thus, overnight, Japan was
deprived of her entire oil supplies.

Now, what were the predestined Inheritors of the Earth
to do? Fight—or quit? The Japanese were not yet ready to
wage a major war—but they were not going to be hounded
into a minor peace. They cheated.

In Washington, ever-smiling Ambassador Admiral Nomura
promised that the Japanese would advance no further into
South-East Asia, and would evacuate Indo-China on the
settlement of the 'China Incident' (see page 20) if, in return,
the United States would renew trade relations.

For the next four months, a pantomime to-and-fro dance
went on in Washington between Japan and the American-
British associates—or, rather let us say, the Almost-Allies,
for the Atlantic Charter had been signed between the United
States and Britain on 12th August 1941. Bluntly, both the
Japanese and the British were playing for time.

It must be said, though, that while the Japs were certainly
seeking to deceive us, it seems that we were only deluding
ourselves. How else can you account for the astonishing
decision made on 29th September 1941, by a top-level con-
ference in Singapore, presided over by Mr Duff Cooper, the
Minister appointed to investigate the whole Far East situa-
tion? For this conference, which included Air Chief Marshal
Sir Robert Brooke-Popham (Commander-in-Chief, Far
East), Vice-Admiral Sir Geoffrey Layton (Commander-in-
Chief, China Station), Sir Shenton Thomas (Governor of the
Straits Settlements and High Commissioner for the Malay
States), the British Ambassador to China, the British
Minister at Bangkok, and the Special Australian Envoy to the
British War Cabinet, agreed that the threat to Singapore
Naval Base was exaggerated because (a) the Japs were con-
centrating against Russia, and (b) any landing in Malaya
was unlikely during the North-east monsoon, which was due
to break in October.

Wrote Winston Churchill himself about this torturing period:

> 'I confess that in my mind the whole Japanese menace lay in a sinister twilight, compared with our other needs. My feeling was that if Japan attacked us, the United States would come in. If the United States did *not* come in, we had no means of defending the Dutch East Indies, or indeed our own Empire in the East. If, on the other hand, Japanese aggression drew in America, I would be content to have it. On this, I rested. . . .'[1]

Meantime, the Japanese were massing for battle. At Saigon, transports were disembarking thousands of troops, who immediately climbed into lorries and drove off westward to the frontier of Siam. Masses of war material rumbled after them. The Japanese Navy was mobilised and, in August, Sir Robert Craigie, British Ambassador in Tokyo, warned No. 10 Downing Street that another move southward by the Japs was imminent.

Now, how much force could they deploy—and how much could we?

At sea, the Japanese Navy, second only to the British and the American in total strength, hopelessly outmatched us in the Far East, where at that moment we did not have a single battleship and barely a handful of destroyers. Nor could we hope for any early improvement. Our naval policy in these distant waters, Churchill frankly admits,[2] was to build up, under the remote cover of the main U.S. Fleet in the Pacific, a really powerful British Eastern Fleet based on Singapore by the spring of 1942.

There was a like disparity in numbers between the land and air forces. Japan's Army mustered 70 field divisions, and she had more than 3,000 first or second line aircraft, many being of very modern design. True, the great mass of these troops, as well as most of the aircraft, were located in Japan or China

---

[1] *The Second World War*. Vol. II. By Winston S. Churchill.
[2] *Ibid.*

but nine or ten divisions were already in Indo-China, as well as about 700 of their planes. The British military forces in Malaya and Singapore during the autumn of 1941 amounted to two-and-a-half weak divisions, and our air strength totalled about 160 planes.

But Japanese superiority lay perhaps even more in quality than in quantity. The troops concentrating for the assault on South-East Asia included the crack 5th and 18th Divisions, especially trained in combined operations, and the Japanese Imperial Guards Division.

Their opposite numbers, responsible for the defence of Malaya and Singapore Island, a country the size of England and Wales (with the Isle of Wight) but mountainous and jungle clad and with much coastal marshland, were a miscellany of British, Australian and Indian troops, together with Malayan Volunteer units. None of the first three had been given any training whatever in jungle fighting before reaching Malaya, and most of them had not been fully trained for any armed combat. Thus General Percival, their Commander-in-Chief:

Of the 27th Australian Infantry Brigade, which arrived in August 1941:

'they had had no training in bush warfare.'

Of the 28th Australian Infantry Brigade, which followed in September: ditto.

Of two field regiments, an anti-tank regiment and a reconnaissance regiment that arrived from India in November:

'excellent material but lacking in experience and with no training in bush warfare. The Indian Recce regiment had only recently been mechanised, and arrived without its armoured vehicles. It was so untrained that drivers had to be borrowed for some of the trucks which were issued to it.'

Of the entire force:

'Apart from the garrison of Singapore Fortress and the Command Reserve . . . there were very few trained units in Malaya in 1941. Throughout the Army there was a serious lack of experienced leaders, the effect of which was accentuated by the inexperience of the troops.'[1]

In the air, the Japanese held supreme advantage. Not for nothing had the German Ambassador at Tokyo, General Ott, flown in from home a thousand expert aeroplane technicians and pilots. They had done their job.

Thus, the Japanese Navy Zero fighter completely outclassed our Brewster Buffalo fighter, which was slow, limited in climb, and with a faulty interrupter gear on its fuselage guns. (These Zeros had obtained an increased range by fitting in auxiliary fuel tanks of aluminium, which could be jettisoned when their load was used up.) Also, the Japanese torpedo-bomber outstripped our Vickers-Vildebeeste, (speed 100 m.p.h., and nicknamed "Flying Coffins") which had been obsolete for more than a year. And the Japanese long range bomber (normal operational height 20,000-24,000 feet and distance 1,600 miles) was superior to our Blenheim. Totally absent from the Royal Air Force in the Far East were any dive-bombers, transport planes, photo-reconnaissance planes and Army co-operation aircraft. There were few trained pilots, and there was also a fearful shortage of spare parts.

A strange story. But stranger, almost incredible, is that of the 'intelligence' both of the Air Ministry and of H.Q., Air Command, Far East.

In May 1941, a Japanese Zero fighter had been shot down in China. Full details of its armament and tankage came through to Singapore and were passed on to the Air Ministry on 26th July 1941, as well as to H.Q., Air Command, Far East. Later, an air attaché in Chungking

---

[1]*Despatches* of Lieut. General Percival.

It is true, however, that the 22nd Australian Infantry Brigade (which had arrived in the spring of 1941) and the 27th Brigade (August arrival) did manage to get in some real jungle training before hostilities opened in December.

sent estimated performance figures, which turned out to be very near the mark. All this was forwarded to the same two authorities before the end of September. But says the official *War Against Japan:*

> 'Faulty organisation at H.Q., Air Command, *whose establishment did not include an Intelligence Staff* (present author's italics) resulted in this valuable report remaining unsifted from the general mass of intelligence information and in no action being taken upon it.' [1]

Meanwhile, at Washington, Japanese Ambassador Admiral Nomura still bowed and smiled as the 'peace' talks proceeded. But over the Far Eastern skies the storm clouds loomed. In Tokyo, the Japanese Foreign Office official newspaper was laying down (5th November 1941) what the United States must do 'or face the alternative.' It included the demand that

> 'Japan's Co-Prosperity Sphere must be acknowledged and Manchukuo, China, Indo-China, Thailand (Siam), the Netherlands East Indies and other States and Protectorates must be allowed to establish their own (*sic*) political and economic relations with Japan without any interference of any kind.'

The Japanese newspaper was thoroughly informed, for that very day the Japanese Imperial Conference decided that unless the United States agreed to their terms by 25th November (no more aid to China, no increase in British and American forces in the Far East, no interference in Indo-China—and also some real co-operation of the United States with Japan to get her the raw materials needed for Japanese industry) then WAR! This message, sent to Japanese embassies overseas, was also decoded.

In Tokyo, and in all big Japanese and Japanese-controlled Chinese and Indo-Chinese cities violent anti-British and anti-American demonstrations were staged.

---

[1] *The War Against Japan*, Vol. 1, by Major General S. Woodburn Kirby, C.B., C.M.G., C.I.E., O.B.E., M.C. H.M. Stationery Office.

In Siam, the people watched with growing dread the movement of Japanese patrols along and across their frontier with Indo-China. They realised that their country was, literally, Japan's next step. Beyond the southern frontier of Siam lay Malaya and Singapore—and those needful oil wells in the islands beyond! In the capital city of Bangkok, and even more particularly in the ports nearest to Malaya, an unusual flood of Japanese travellers suddenly developed. Warned the Bangkok radio:

> 'Get ready for war! Learn how to fight under competent authorities!'

On 20th November, Japan delivered her 'final word' to Washington. This proposed her own evacuation of Indo-China, pending a general settlement with China or 'the restoration of peace in the Pacific'—when she would clear out from China entirely. In return, that oil please!

On 26th November, the United States Government replied with a Ten Point Note, requiring the Japanese to withdraw all military, naval, air force and police forces from both Indo-China and China. There was to be no further support for any Chinese régime except the National Government, headed by General Chiang Kai-Shek, at Chungking.

But far closer on the ball than any of these diplomatic exchanges was the significant signal which had reached British Headquarters in the Far East the previous day, 25th November, by roundabout route from Tokyo. It read:

> 'Railway carriage windows for Japanese and foreigners alike are screened for the whole length of the Inland Sea.'

It was plain that some considerable operation was being mounted.

About this time, there came repeated reports of Japanese planes flying high over the mountains of Malaya and of Borneo. (Indeed, according to Japanese sources, their land-based attack bombers patrolled the seas a hundred miles

South of Singapore).[1] Also, four cruisers with attendant destroyers reinforced the Japanese Fleet in the harbours of Indo-China. Still more significant, a convoy of landing craft made off from the Japanese-occupied ports of China to destinations unknown.

On the night of 29th November, notices flashed on the cinema screens of Singapore and other towns of Malaya.

> 'All British and Australian Imperial Forces to report immediately to their units.'

A War Office cable had been received, warning that the Washington talks might break down and that the Japanese might launch an invasion of Siam, the Dutch East Indies and the Philippines. A state of 'Second Degree Readiness' was ordered and the Volunteer Forces mobilised. Also, air reconnaissance over the Gulf of Siam and the South China Sea was undertaken.

Next day, came dramatic confirmation of Japanese duplicity. This was another Tokyo-Berlin signal to the Japanese Ambassador in Germany, which had been picked up by our Intelligence on 30th November. It instructed him to speak with Hitler and von Ribbentrop and to

> 'Say very secretly to them that there is extreme danger that war may suddenly break out between the Anglo-Saxon nations and Japan through some clash of arms, and add that the time of the breaking out of this war may come quicker than anyone dreams.'

Again, the alarm signals were flashed to British Service Commanders. They were 'AWAKE!' (International situation getting worse) and 'ARMOUR!' (Man defence of vulnerable points).

In fact, though *this* was not disclosed in the Tokyo-Berlin messages, the Japanese Fleet to attack Pearl Harbour had actually sailed on 25th November. It could, of course, have

[1]See '*Zero.*' The Story of the Japanese Navy Air Force. 1937-1945. By Masatake Okumiya & Jiro Horikoshi with Martin Caidin (Cassell & Co., Ltd.)

Australian anti-tank gunners on a jungle road block in Malaya firing at point-blank range against the advancing enemy tanks

The Johore Causeway which linked Singapore Island with the mainland of Malaya. It was only partially destroyed by the British during the retreat

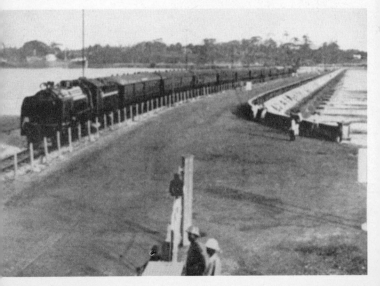

Seafront of Singapore City during the war

been signalled to suspend action, but on 1st December (as we know now) at the Imperial Conference held in Tokyo, the final decision was made to go to war—*AND WHEN!*

The orders flashed to the Fleet Commander, Admiral Nagumo:

> 'The date for the declaration of war is fixed for December 8.'

That very day, in London, General Sir Alan Brooke, who had just been appointed Chief of Imperial General Staff in succession to General Sir John Dill, was summoned to No. 10 Downing St. to discuss the possibilities of forestalling a Japanese invasion of Siam.

Now History was marching—at the double. On 2nd December, there sailed into the great Naval Base at Singapore the newest British battleship H.M.S. *Prince of Wales*, with the battle-cruiser H.M.S. *Repulse* and four destroyers. They had been dispatched there on the personal insistence of the Prime Minister, Winston Churchill, in a last effort to deter the Japanese from their wild adventure. It is possible that they impressed, or at any rate, pleased the *Tuans Besar* (the British and European merchant princes) of this rich, sprawling city—though it did not stir them to any further effort in their own sadly neglected Civil Defence. No double-marching for *Tuans!*

Wrote O. D. Gallagher, the *Daily Express* War Correspondent, of Singapore at this hour:

> 'With a few exceptions, the white civilian population evinced no interest in the war whatsoever, except at the breakfast table when papers, reporting news from the battlefronts of Russia and North Africa, gave them something exciting to chatter about.'

And Gallagher's impressions seem to have been shared by others. Wrote an Australian officer after the war (he had reached Singapore earlier that year of 1941, but obviously nothing much had changed in the following months):

B

'I still have very vivid memories of my first mental reactions on our arrival in Singapore. We were being sent to a war station. We were equipped—even if only 50% equipped—for war. Yet the first sight that met our eyes on the first evening was officers in mess dress and fashionable women in evening dress. It was not only incongruous, it was wrong. Either we were crazy, or they were crazy. Either there was danger, or there was no danger. If the latter, why had we been sent there, and why were more troops on the way from India?'[1]

Up until the very hour that the first Jap bombs showered down on Singapore City the gay, luxurious social life continued there—tennis, golf, cricket, bathing, boating during the daytime, and crowded cocktail, theatre and dinner parties far into the night. By the way, except at top level, the various 'colours' did not easily mix together. (It must be added that the Aussies themselves got on extremely well with the native Malays).

It was during the early days of December 1941 that an almost incredible thing happened to Lieut. General Gordon Bennett, Commander of the Australian Imperial Force in Malaya. By direct arrangement with his own Government he had been on a brief tour of the Australian divisions in the Middle East. Returning to Cairo from the Western Desert on 3rd December, he quotes from his diary that he

'was handed a cable from Malaya saying that Malaya Command considers that there is no need for me to rush back as things are quiet and there is no prospect of hostilities.'[2]

It appears that this cable came from the A.I.F. for it certainly did not come from Malaya Command. In any event, General Bennett decided to push on.

[1] See *The Japanese Thrust* by Lionel Wigmore (Australian War Memorial: The Griffin Press, Adelaide, Australia).

[2] In his book *Why Singapore Fell*, by Lt. General H. Gordon Bennett. Angus & Robertson, Ltd., 1944.

The North-east monsoon storm was now blowing off the shores of Malaya. Under that cloud blanket the accurate 'spotting' of ships by reconnaissance pilots is not very easy work. Nevertheless, about noon of 6th December Flight Lieut. J. C. Ramshaw, flying a Hudson plane of No. 1 Squadron Royal Australian Air Force saw a motor vessel and two minelayers about 200 miles off Kota Bharu, the northernmost port of Malaya. Half-an-hour later, and he had added to his 'bag' a battleship, five cruisers, seven destroyers and about 25 merchantmen, almost certainly troop transports. About 1 o'clock, a second Hudson reported another convoy of two cruisers, 10 destroyers and about 20 merchantmen. This Hudson was chased by a Japanese plane.

Now the first few ships had been sailing on a north-westerly course into the Gulf of Siam as though bound for Bangkok. *But the two convoys were moving due West.* At this point, comes the greatest mystery of all. The Commander-in-Chief, Far East, Air Chief Marshal Sir Robert Brooke-Popham, decided to do nothing, except order a 'First Degree of Readiness!' It was not Malaya but Siam which was going to be invaded. So, none of our business!

Writes General Percival:

> 'The Command was at the fullest degree of readiness, but there was no undue alarm, owing to the view that the Japanese expedition was directed against Siam.'[1]

Next day, more Hudsons, later relieved by Catalinas, were ordered off to shadow the convoys. But in the thick, muzzy weather they failed ever to make contact again. A Catalina, despatched on reconnaissance at 2 a.m. on this morning of 7th December, never returned. We learnt later that it had been shot down. About 6.30 that evening, that is, 30 hours after the first convoy had been sighted, reconnaissance reports began flowing in of a Japanese cruiser sailing West and of four destroyers, with a merchantman loaded with men in khaki uniforms on its decks *sailing South.*

[1]See his *Despatches.*

By the way, at 11 a.m. that same morning, the Japanese Ambassador in Siam had delivered an ultimatum, demanding free passage through that country for Japanese troops, planes, etc. Neither the British Legation nor British Intelligence appeared to have heard of it. Now night fell.

Midnight! One o'clock! Then, signals came crowding in to Singapore from North Malaya. Japanese warships were shelling the coastal defences near Kota Bharu. Japanese planes were bombing the airfields in all the northern provinces. Japanese assault barges were landing troops.

Two o'clock! Three! Four! Then, in Singapore the air raid sirens howled. H.Q. A.R.P. was not even manned, though on 1st December another—and still more urgent—warning signal 'ALBERT!' (watch for hostile aircraft) had gone out. Every street light was still glowing—and remained so. Half-an-hour later police, A.R.P. and Power Station officials were still scouring the town for the one man who had the key of the central switch for the blackout. (It should be recorded that only two practice blackouts had ever been held in Singapore, during the previous September).

Can this haywire state of affairs possibly be explained? Yes. The Civil Defence of Singapore was under the Civil Administration and no effective link-up had ever been made between them and the Armed Services.[1]

4.30 a.m.! In droned the Japanese bombers. One wave, in a formation of nine flew over without bombing—to draw the searchlights and ack-ack guns off the following ones. They flew, the first lot, at 12,000 feet; the second at 4,000 feet. Mainly, their targets were the harbour and the airfields beyond the town, though a number of bombs crashed into the streets. It was the first knowledge that the population had that war had broken out in the Far East.

Our own Brewster Buffalo fighters made no challenge in the sky to the invading enemy bombers. They stayed grounded—so as not to interfere with our ack-ack gunfire.

Five o'clock! Then, the signal, 'Raiders Passed.'

[1] Nor was any link-up made until several more days had elapsed. See page 90.

The disastrous battle for Malaya and Singapore had begun. After 10 years warning and the trumpet sounds of the last few hours, in surprise, muddle and alarm for the defenders. The story of the Red Light that wasn't noticed.

Why?

CHAPTER THREE

OVER THE LINE

By dawn, 8th December, the battle for all South-East Asia had taken shape.

Already, on the previous day, a vast raid of carrier-borne planes from Japan had sunk the United States Pacific Fleet as it lay anchored in Pearl Harbour. Then, a little later, a Japanese bombing attack on Manila, in the Philippine Islands, had practically wiped out the American aircraft grounded there. About the same hour, Singapore had received its own blitz baptism (it is 16 hours behind Pearl Harbour in time). Meanwhile, of course, the airfields of North Malaya had also been raked by fire from the skies, and Japanese assault troops had come ashore near by.

This happened soon after midnight, 7/8th December, on the North-east coast beyond Kota Bharu, about 10 miles from the Siamese border. Half-an-hour earlier, Beach Defence troops of 31/7*Dogra Regt. had reported ships anchoring and sending off assault barges. Our artillery opened fire, and sank several of the incoming craft, but it also drew down upon the defences some heavy shelling from the guns of the enemy warships. By 1 a.m. the invaders had captured the wired and mined line of the nearest pillboxes, at the cost of very high casualties to themselves ; as for our tough little Dogra garrison, it was wiped out to a man.

Meantime, our Hudson planes, in the face of fierce ack-ack volleys, repeatedly attacked the Japanese ships that night, though with what success is not known. (It seems likely

* Should be 3/17   38

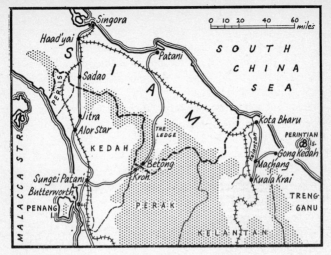

that it was these bombs which set alight one of their transports).

With morning, came reinforcement of R.A.F. Vildebeeste torpedo-bombers (Nos. 36 and 100 Squadrons) and R.A.A.F. Buffalo fighters (No. 1 Squadron). On the sandy beaches, and along the nipah palm-covered banks and creeks of Kelantan River, they took toll of many an enemy-laden landing craft. But low clouds at sea masked the daylight withdrawal of the Japanese warships and transports to behind the Perintian Islands, 15 miles offshore.

Northward, 80 miles over the border to the Siamese port of Patani, where another Japanese landing had been reported, flew R.A.F. Blenheims (No. 62 Squadron), and they certainly located some enemy ships there still busily disembarking troops, though they were held off from them by a greatly superior fighter cover of Zeros. Our planes flew back to their own base at Alor Star, in the north-western Malay State of Kedah, to re-fuel.

Hardly had they landed when the enemy counterblast came in, a pattern-bombing attack (partly high explosive and partly incendiary) delivered from 12,000 feet by more than a score of

Japanese Army '97' twin-engine bombers. Then low-fliers scythed along the airfield, machine-gunning. By one means or another, ten of our Blenheims were hit (we were left with only two serviceable planes in all), buildings and fuel dumps were set afire, and the controlled water supply system smashed.

That same day, as the monsoon rain flooded down in sheets, the Japanese launched further air onslaughts against the neighbouring airfields at Sungei Patani, Butterworth, and Penang Island on the West coast, as well as against Kota Bharu, Gong Kedah and Machang, which are fairly closely grouped together on the East coast. Wrote General Percival of these events:

> 'The performance of the Japanese aircraft of all types and the accuracy of their high level bombing had come as an unpleasant surprise. Our own Air Force had already been seriously weakened.'[1]

The seaborne invasion also went on. Soon after the departure of our searching planes from the seas off Kota Bharu, more Japanese troopships turned up, escorted by a cruiser and several destroyers, to reinforce that savage Battle of the Beach.

By 4 p.m. the invaders had fought their way ashore, and reports came in that they were approaching the boundary of the airfield. Japanese fighter patrols already commanded the sky above it. In the temporary absence of the Station Commander (Group Captain Noble), his deputy having decided that it could no longer be made available for our own operations, sought and obtained leave from the Air Force H.Q. in Singapore to evacuate (if he could!) the remaining serviceable planes by air southward to Kelantan, the ground staff and stores being shifted by road to the railhead. On the Station Commander's return, he found that the alarm had been a false one—or, rather, premature. For as dusk closed in, the Japs did draw near the airfield. In the gathering

[1] See his *Despatches*.

gloom and a pelting storm, the last of our aircraft flew off.

That night, Brigadier B. W. Key, D.S.O., M.C., Commander of the 'Kelantan Force' (as the troops defending this threshold of Kelantan State were called), found that Japanese infiltrations through the swampy labyrinth of the river and the shallow creeks along the shore were threatening his position. He therefore ordered retirement to a line South of Kota Bharu, on the right bank.

In the confused din of battle, amid the jungle trees and scrub, the dreary pad-pad through the slime and stench, and the shadows of the night, orders went astray and part of his 1st Frontier Force Rifles were left behind, a grim foretoken of what was to happen again and again in this rout and retreat of seventy days and nights to Singapore.

Thus, writes General Percival,

> 'Within 24 hours of the start of the campaign, the Japanese had gained their first major objective, but at considerable cost. It is believed that the forces landed in Kelantan consisted of rather less than one Japanese division. This force lost its accompanying tank formation and many of its guns before it got ashore.'[1]

But by this time, a Japanese invasion fork of at least three prongs was driving down into Malaya, towards Singapore.

How had this major operation happened?

It is time, at this point, to consider its development. For Japan's Operation Malaya was an integral, unavoidable part of her Operation Singapore, the capture of the greatest naval base in the Far East.

It was not always deemed to be so. Almost up to the outbreak of World War II, the security of Singapore Naval Base rested on the power of the Royal Navy to command the surrounding seas. The nearest Japanese base of any kind in those days was still about 2,000 miles away, which placed the

[1]See *Despatches*.

target beyond the range of their existing aircraft. Unless, therefore, they could seize some more adjacent territory, the Japanese would have to rely on carrier-borne planes to launch an air attack.

But when the Second World War had actually begun, with Britain's inevitable commitments in Europe severely restricting our naval resources in the Far East, this strategical set-up sharply changed.

It must be recorded that Mr. Churchill's fundamental views did not. Thus, on 10th September 1940, the Prime Minister was writing to General Ismay, the Deputy Secretary (Military) to the War Cabinet:

> 'The prime defence of Singapore is the Fleet . . . the fact that the Japanese had made landings in Malaya, and had even begun the siege of the Fortress would not deprive a superior relieving fleet of its power. On the contrary, the plight of the besiegers, cut off from home while installing themselves in the swamps of the jungles, would be all the more forlorn. The defence of Singapore must, therefore, be based upon a strong local garrison and the general potentialities of sea power. . . . The probabilities of the Japanese undertaking an attack on Singapore, which would involve so large a proportion of their Fleet far outside the Yellow Sea are remote; in fact, nothing can be more foolish from their point of view. Far more attractive are the Dutch East Indies.'[1]

This was a curious estimate of the nature of a possible Japanese attack, since even before the Second World War began in 1939, the Committee of Imperial Defence had increased the period before relief could reach Singapore from Britain by sea from 70 days to 90. In 1940, the Chiefs of Staff raised it further to 180 days. Yet on 22nd November of that year, Mr Churchill in a letter to Mr A. V. Alexander, First Lord of the Admiralty was re-emphasising:

[1] See *The Second World War*, Vol. II. By Winston S. Churchill.

'The Japanese Navy is not likely to venture far from its home base so long as a superior Battle Fleet is maintained at Singapore or at Honolulu. The Japanese would never attempt a siege of Singapore with a hostile, superior American fleet in the Pacific.'[1]

But, of course, by November 1941, a year later, Britain had still no battle fleet at Singapore—and, within a few days more, the United States had none at Honolulu.

Theirs, it is true, had only vanished overnight in the hurricane blitz of the Japanese against Pearl Harbour, in the Pacific Ocean. Ours was then in the other seas of the world, fighting the Germans in the Atlantic Ocean and the Mediterranean. But, in fact, no British Fleet had ever been at Singapore in all the 20 years since it was first decided to build that £63,000,000 Naval Base there.

Nor were other vital elements of the defence plan ever carried out. Thus, while the 'relief period' for Fortress Singapore had been raised from about two months to six months, it had always been proposed that as much as six months' supply of food, etc. should be stocked there for the garrison and the civil population. No provision on this scale had been even set in hand when the blow fell in December 1941.

In fact, almost nothing was done to bring that defence plan up-to-date. The 12th Indian Infantry Brigade group was dispatched from India to Malaya, but the idea was still to hold only Singapore Island and the approaches to it in the State of Johore, southernmost part of the Malayan mainland. This took no account of the vastly increased range of aircraft since 1921, which had opened up Singapore to attack by carrier-borne and shore-based planes from far greater distances.

Indeed, it was Percival himself, then a Staff Officer in Malaya Command, who in 1937 had drawn up an appreciation and a plan for a Japanese attack on Singapore, and

[1]*Ibid.*

handed it over to the War Office on his return to England that very autumn.

Percival had done this as a result of observing Japanese troops practising combined operations on the China coast, 'with no lack of special landing craft.' Also, he had noted building in the Japanese shipyards a fleet of 18-knot merchant ships, but with deck space for passengers rather than for cargo—*why?*

Percival pointed out that as a result of the tensing political situation in Europe and the unlikelihood of the British Fleet reaching Singapore in the 70 days then contemplated, a much more deliberate form of attack could be launched than we had so far imagined. His own belief was that the Japanese would seize airfields in Southern Siam and Northern Malaya, occupy the harbours of Borneo, then stage their final assault on Singapore.[1]

It is pretty clear, however, that well before the curtain rose on World War II it had been accepted by the Imperial Defence Authorities that Singapore could not be held if the Malayan mainland fell. In May 1938, Maj. General W. G. S. Dobbie, then General Officer Commanding, Malaya, had written:

'It is an attack from the Northward that I regard as the greatest potential danger to the Fortress. Such attack could be carried out during the period of the North-east monsoon. *The jungle is not in most places impassable for infantry*' (Author's italics).

In April 1940, Lieut. General L. V. Bond, who had succeeded Dobbie in the Malaya Command, inclined to the view

[1] Winston Churchill himself came very near to this estimate more than three years later, in a letter to President Roosevelt, 15th February 1941.

'I do not myself think that the Japanese would be likely to send the large military expedition necessary to lay siege to Singapore. The Japanese would no doubt occupy whatever strategic points and oilfields in the Dutch East Indies and thereabouts that they covet, and thus get a far better position for a full-scale attack on Singapore later on. They would also raid Australian and New Zealand ports and coasts, causing deep anxiety in those Dominions, which had already sent all their best trained fighting men to the Far East.'

(See *The Second World War.* Vol. II. By Winston S. Churchill.)

that the Japanese attack would be launched from South Siam, and reckoned that the frontier line could be held for several months. He set the defence force required at four infantry divisions, three machine-gun battalions, and a couple of tank regiments. If this was not possible—and provided adequate R.A.F. strength could be made available— then rather less than three divisions, plus some anti-tank batteries and armoured cars would do, conceded General Bond.

Now, what would be 'adequate' R.A.F. support? The Commanders on the spot reckoned that it should be around 566 first-line aircraft. But in August 1940, the Chiefs of Staff Committee slashed this figure to a minimum of 336 first-line aircraft. Every effort would be made to supply these by the end of 1941. In the meantime, they agreed that our Land Forces must amount to at least three divisions.

Two months later, at a Singapore Defence Conference, attended by representatives of Great Britain, Australia, New Zealand, India and Burma (with a United States observer) the aircraft total was raised again to 566 planes. The Chiefs of Staff Committee, in London, once more refused to accept this new figure, though they agreed that when the 336 planes had been provided the Army strength should remain as it was.

It was at this time that there was devised that famous military operation known as 'MATADOR.' The plan was that, having thoroughly assured ourselves *when* the enemy intended to land in Southern Siam for the invasion of Malaya, a British expeditionary force (drawn from the 11th Indian Infantry Division, then stationed in North Malaya) should cross the frontier 24 hours ahead of them and be awaiting them on the beaches. It was thought that the invaders would seek to come ashore on the East coast at Singora and also, possibly, at Patani (which was, in the event, exactly where they did land). There is a port at Singora, and there are airfields at both places. To deny them to the enemy, even if we could not use them ourselves, would be a thoroughly worthwhile job.

Now, there are two roads and two railways from South Siam into North Malaya. A main road and a railway run from Singora, via Haad' yai Junction, into the westerly State of Kedah. A secondary road runs from Patani into the adjoining State of Perak, while another railway branches off at Haad' yai Junction along the East Coast into the State of Kelantan.

So, if we could grab that Haad' yai key point, we might be able to press on to Singora—and also to switch aside down the railway in the direction of Patani. (The only other way to reach Patani would be by sending a separate force up that secondary road from the State of Perak).

It was realised that in making our dash forward we should certainly have to watch out lest the Siamese themselves destroyed the bridges which span the ravines of that thickly-forested mountain land. (By the way, the recent reconstruction and widening of main road bridges in South Siam had not escaped our attention; we knew who was urging this on— and why!)

Part of the preparation for coming events, which we shared with our future opponents in them, was the reconnaissance carried out in South Siam by officers in plain clothes. Both British and Japanese were busy at it, and so many were the visitors that they often met and even stayed together at the same rest-houses, hotels and inns, such as the German-owned Zoo Hotel in Haad' yai. Like us, too, no doubt the Japanese were also printing maps, banknotes in Siamese currency, and pamphlets in that language for distribution when the lid should at last blow off the cauldron.

Other preliminaries were the building of defensive positions, pill-boxes, gun sites and anti-tank barriers at cross-roads and on airfields. So much had to be done, so little local or service labour was available, and so heavy were the monsoon rains that the troops themselves had to divide their time between this sapper work and their jungle battle training—with the result that both suffered.

For a critical issue which was never settled was this: *the priority of Malaya's functions in the British Empire's War effort.*

Producing half of the world output of tin and one-third of the rubber, Malaya certainly earned Sir Shenton Thomas's description of it as a 'dollar arsenal' (i.e. $135,000,000 in the second eleven months of the war compared with $98,000,000 in the first year). So, was the production of these raw materials of more vital importance than the training and sustaining of the forces, regular and volunteer, in Malaya? Was it more useful to have more Malayan, Indian and Chinese labourers working in the tin mines and on the rubber plantations than digging trenches or building pill-boxes—and the resident British managers, technicians and clerks engaged in industrial and commercial operations, or serving as Territorial officers in the various Malay Volunteer Units? A cable from Whitehall to Sir Shenton instructed him that

> 'the ultimate criterion for exemption (from military service) should be not what the General Officer Commanding considers practicable, but what you consider essential to maintain the necessary production and efficient labour management.'[1]

Now, right on the important strategic road that led from Patani into the State of Perak there arose a military engineering problem. Here, at the frontier town called Kroh, the road forked westward and southward. To cover the approach effectively it was necessary to go into Siam but, of course, no defence works could be created there while peace still officially reigned. A key question was: *How swiftly could the job be done the day that war broke out?*

The site we really wanted, by the way, was about 40 miles beyond the frontier, known as 'The Ledge,' where the road had been hacked out of the cliffside. If we could not reach

[1]See *The Japanese Thrust* above.

Patani in time to meet the incoming Japanese assault wave (or, then, contain it), surely a resolute party could grab, fortify and hold 'The Ledge'?

Indeed, there was exactly such a party ready for that task. It was the mobile column called 'Krohcol,' which consisted of the 3/16th Punjab Regiment, a battery of Federated Malay States Volunteers and a company of sappers. Krohcol was commanded by Lieut. Colonel H. D. Moorhead.

Such was Operation MATADOR. *What happened to it?*

Up to 5th December 1941, it had been forbidden to mount Operation MATADOR without authority from the War Cabinet. Indeed, the most explicit instructions had been issued to all our Civil and Military establishments in the Far East to

'avoid war with Japan.'

But, on this day, the Commander-in-Chief Far East, Air Chief Marshal Sir Robert Brooke-Popham, told General Percival that he had received permission to put MATADOR into effect at once, without further reference to London. He had to be satisfied himself about two questions.

(i) Was a Japanese expedition moving towards South Siam? (ii) Had the Japanese violated any other part of Siam?[1]

It will be recalled how, the very next morning, our air reconnaissance sighted Japanese warships sailing westward into the Gulf of Siam, and also how subsequently both Japanese warships and troopships were reported to be at sea. But still MATADOR waited.

Says Brooke-Popham, defending this astonishing delay:

'the main reason being that at least 24 hours start was required before the anticipated time of a Japanese landing, and this was most unlikely to be available should the ships seen turn out to be part of a Japanese expedition. Further, the conditions for reconnaissance were

---

[1] *Despatches* of Air Chief Marshal Sir Robert Brooke-Popham, G.C.V.O., K.C.B., C.M.G., D.S.O., A.F.C.

bad, and on the information available there could be no certainty that the Japanese were about to open hostilities, and on more than one occasion the British Minister to Thailand (Siam) had stressed the serious consequences that would ensue should we be the first to break Thai neutrality.

It is pertinent to add that until the Japanese had committed some definite act of hostility against the United States, the Dutch or ourselves, permission had not been given to attack a Japanese expedition at sea.'[1]

So, on that night of 7/8th December, while the Japanese Commandoes waded or swam ashore from their assault barges under British fire on the sands of Kota Bharu, in Malaya (and disembarked entirely undisturbed, in parade ground order, from their transports on to the quays and jetties of Singora and Patani in Siam), the troops of 11th Indian Division, spearhead of Operation MATADOR, champed and fretted under a drenching downpour in their camps near the frontier.

For soon after midnight, the 'buzz' ran round the tents and the *bashas* that the enemy was already on the move. At 11.20 p.m., after a council of war in G.H.Q. Far East, Singapore, when MATADOR was put back on ice once more, Lieut. General Sir L. Heath, commanding the 3rd Indian Corps (of which 11th Indian Division was a part) had been told of the decision. But, at the same time, he had been warned that MATADOR might be ordered into effect if need be, at dawn.

So, Corps H.Q. rang up Division H.Q. to say 'Hold everything—but be ready to move off within half-an-hour!' It was not long before the telephone exchanges rattled again—and they kept going all night long while the news poured in of the landings.

At 8.20 a.m. on the morning of 8th December, G.H.Q. Far East reported that MATADOR had been approved by the

[1]*Ibid.*

Chiefs of Staff Committee in London if the Japanese attacked Kota Bharu, which they *had* done nine hours earlier. But General Percival was still ordered by G.H.Q. Far East, 'Do not act!' So, finally buried, was that Operation that might have changed the fate of the War in the Far East.

Now, Percival confined himself, as he says, to authorising

'certain harassing activities which had been planned, and also to lay demolition charges on the roads and railways.'[1]

There chanced to be a meeting in Singapore at 10 a.m. that same morning of the Straits Settlements Legislative Council, so General Percival thought he would snatch a few minutes off to look in there and tell

'these representatives of the people some first-hand information of what was really going on. Everybody was quite calm. Even in Singapore itself, apart from a few groups of people discussing the news, there was no outward sign that anything abnormal was happening.'[2]

An hour later, returning to his own headquarters, Percival received permission from G.H.Q. Far East to move troops into Siamese territory if he judged fit. Promptly, he telephoned to Lieut. General Heath, ordering him to dispatch mobile forces across the frontier to occupy the selected defensive positions, cover the main approaches, and to harass and delay the enemy. But, at the same time, in marshalling the defence forces behind the frontier, Percival had actually to muster back to the crossroads at Jitra, in the hilly northlands of the State of Kedah, those troops who had already been set moving. These were a couple of battalions of 11th Indian Division which had been sent to the entraining stations the previous day for that now abandoned MATADOR dash on Haad' yai Junction.

[1] See *Despatches*.
[2] See his book.

'This change,' he writes, 'from an anticipated offensive, for which the 11th Indian Division had been energetically preparing for some weeks, to the defensive had undoubtedly a considerable psychological effect on the troops.'[1]

It was not until late afternoon that the first British troops crossed the frontier, two companies of the 1/8th Punjab Regiment and a detachment of sappers, with carriers and some anti-tank guns. These units were part of another mobile column commanded by Brigadier W. O. Lay, D.S.O., and known as 'Laycol'.

By dusk, which falls about 6.30 p.m. at this time of year, they had reached the village of Sadao, about 9 miles North of the frontier, where they encamped in a ring round the huts. Three hours later, lights gleamed through the torrential downpour and the darkness of the forest. They were the headlamps of a column of Japanese tanks, followed by truckloads of infantry.

Lieut. May, in charge of the anti-tank battery, held his fire until the leading tank was within a hundred yards. Then he ordered his gunners to open up, which they did with prompt effect. The first, second and third tanks were halted, and knocked out. The lorries behind them piled up, and the Punjabi riflemen swept them with fire.

But swiftly, the Japanese infantry debussed on either side of the road, and began to encircle our position. At the same time, they brought their mortars into action. It was by the light of the blazing wreckage on the roadside that our men spotted the shadowy figures moving through the trees and shrubbery on our right flank.

Now, the British sappers were ready to blow the bridges which lay in our rear. The order was given to retire, the echoing blast of several explosions followed, and before the enemy realised that we were gone, three broken bridges lay between us. As 'Laycol' Force re-crossed the frontier, they

---

[1]See *Despatches*.

learned a British armoured train party had gone up the rail-way towards Singora and destroyed a 200-foot girder bridge before retiring. It seriously messed-up Japanese transport for many weeks.

The adventures of Lieut. Colonel Moorhead's 'Krohcol' were less happy.

At 1.30 p.m. on that opening day of battle, 8th December, Moorhead had received his orders to move across the frontier and seize The Ledge. With a force of far less than prescribed strength (he had been able to muster only one battalion, i.e. his own 3/16th Punjab Regiment, and an Australian Reserve M.T. Company for transport), Moorhead set off at once. Reaching the padlocked frontier gate on the Kroh-Patani road, our scouts smashed it open with axes. But as the leading scout marched through he was shot dead by Siamese rifle fire.

Or was it Japanese—the sons of Nippon being dressed in the uniforms of Siamese Armed Constabulary?

For as our carrier platoon led the column forward, at every bend along the twisting jungle track there were am-bushes and road blocks. Snipers perched in the trees, or lay in the thick bracken on the roadside within a hand's touch or a kick of the marching men.

Often, they let the scouts and the advance guard go by, then opened fire on the main body or on the road-clearing parties. Our flanking squads had to cut their way through the jungle bramble to get at them, and twice they rose and charged us with fixed bayonets. By nightfall, Krohcol had advanced only three miles towards The Ledge, at a cost of 15 casualties to themselves and 24 to the enemy. They halted, and made camp, ringing it with patrols. All night long, sniping went on.

At dawn, Moorhead led his force off again—to the same kind of fighting, against 'Siamese policemen,' who this time were reinforced by several dozen convicts released from a near-by prison. It was not until early afternoon that they reached the village of Betong, about six miles further on. Here, suddenly, white flags were flown (a huge one had been nailed to the concrete arch in the village centre), firing ceased and a Siamese official came forward and courteously apologised for the 'mistake' which the police had made. It is not known why Moorhead did not push on to The Ledge, but the delay proved fatal.

Next morning, as our lorry-borne troops approached it, two Japanese planes flew along the road and dropped bombs, without doing effective damage. Advancing now on foot along the road through a ravine above the roaring Patani river, about 2 p.m. our Punjabi infantry came under fire again. No doubt as to the enemy this time! This was the crack Japanese 5th Division, who had moved up from Patani.

A ferocious encounter battle ensued, in which the Japanese deployed tanks and mountain artillery. Fighting went on into the night, much of it hand-to-hand and knife-to-knife, continuing all next day. Krohcol had now been in action for four days, and the fourth night was coming up. By this time it was plain that the force could not fight their way forward to The Ledge. Casualties had been heavy, almost every man in some companies being either killed or wounded. In close combat, indeed, the Punjabis outmatched the Japanese but enemy total strength much outnumbered ours, although on this last night of the Battle for The Ledge reinforcements reached us from the 5/14th Punjab Regiment.

Moorhead made up his mind to fall back towards the frontier with the gallant remnant and signalled to Divisional H.Q. for permission. Having obtained it, he held on for the night, planning to move out at dawn. By then, the enemy was already in full assault again, and had almost outflanked us. Only some furious bayonet counter-attacks drove him back.

We had only four carriers left. Moorhead ordered the derelicts to be jacked on to the sodden track as barriers, himself supervising the job under continual fire. He was the last man to leave with the rearguard as they pulled out that morning, back towards Betong, jumping aboard the rearmost carrier.

As he did so, he saw a wounded Punjabi lance-naik about

50 yards away, lifting a weary hand of farewell. Moorhead leapt out of the carrier, ran back along the bullet-swept and shell-blasted road to pick him up, put him on his shoulder and bear him to the carrier.

So ended the Battle for The Ledge.

Now, the Frontier War was on. But already tragic disaster had fallen on the British flag. The battleship *Prince of Wales* and the battlecruiser *Repulse* had been sunk off the shores of Malaya, and the command of the seas, vital to the defence of the country and of Fortress Singapore, had passed into the hands of the enemy.

CHAPTER FOUR

THE LOST SHIPS

IT was on the evening of the first day of war in Malaya that Rear-Admiral Sir Tom Phillips, Commander-in-Chief of the newly set up Far Eastern Fleet, resolved that the Royal Navy must play a positive part during these hours of decision.

He had flown to Singapore only the previous morning from Manila, where he had been discussing possible joint action with Lieut. General Douglas MacArthur, who as commander of the United States Army Forces in the Far East, was in charge of the Philippine Army, and Admiral Hart, who commanded the United States Asiatic Fleet. Indeed, Admiral Phillips had arrived back at Singapore just in time to take part in the conference when, for the last time, Operation MATADOR was postponed.

All next day, came reports of the fighting and bombing in North Malaya. Phillips felt that the vague deterrent power on the enemy's naval intentions of the newly-arrived battleship *Prince of Wales*, and battlecruiser *Repulse*, was not enough while they merely remained in the Naval Base at Singapore. He reckoned that they could take active part in repelling those invasions from the Gulf of Siam. He and his officers were convinced that the *Prince of Wales*, with her radar-controlled ack-ack guns ('Chicago pianos') was unsinkable.

So Admiral Sir Tom Phillips swiftly organised what was named 'Force Z,' consisting of the *Prince of Wales*, the

Repulse, and the four destroyers *Electra*, *Express*, *Vampire* and *Tenedos*. This fleet left Singapore about 5.30 p.m. on 8th December, and set forth on a northerly course.

According to O. D. Gallagher, the *Daily Express* War Correspondent, who sailed in the *Repulse* on this foredoomed voyage, Force Z moved out to sea that evening watched by several hundreds of people on shore. He wrote, afterwards:

> 'I have wondered since if there were any Japanese agents among them with access to small portable radio-transmitters.'[1]

General Percival believes that it is more than likely that this was done by the secret enemy wireless sets which throughout the campaign transmitted messages from the Singapore-Johore area to the Japanese lines, defying all efforts to locate them.

Before sailing off, Admiral Phillips asked the Air Officer Commanding Far East, Air Vice-Marshal C. W. H. Pulford, for three services.

(1) Reconnaissance 100 miles North of Force Z, from dawn on 9th December; (2) reconnaissance to Singora and beyond, ten miles off the coast, from dawn on 10th December; (3) fighter protection off Singora, from dawn on 10th December.

To these requests, Pulford replied that as for (1), he could provide. About (2), he was hopeful though doubtful, because the Blenheim planes which would have to do the job were based on Kuantan airfield, half-way up the East Coast of Malaya, and it was uncertain if this airfield would still be in action then. As for (3), this was definitely impossible, because the northern airfields were either already untenable or else had been devastated by bombing.

So our short-range Buffalo fighters would have to operate from distant bases, which would seriously curtail their combat-time before they must return and refuel. In any event,

---

[1] *Retreat in the East*. By O. D. Gallagher (George Harrap & Co., Ltd. London).

we were desperately hard up for fighters, even to defend Singapore.

The Fleet was already at sea when Air Vice-Marshal Pulford's reply came back from R.A.F. H.Q. So the signal was made to Admiral Phillips aboard the *Prince of Wales*, and duly acknowledged. A later signal confirmed that no fighter cover could be provided off the Siam coast.

Next day, 9th December, the weather favoured the mission of Force Z, with grey, low cloud, drizzling rain and visibility almost nil. But already at first light, had come an unconfirmed report from the destroyer *Vampire* of a Japanese plane, sighted by a single look-out man for a minute.

Meantime, spirits were high in the two British battleships. Both had taken part in the memorable chase earlier that year of the German giant dreadnought, *Bismarck*, though only the *Prince of Wales* had been in the final battle. *The Prince of Wales* had also served in the Malta convoys, as well as carrying Prime Minister Churchill across the Atlantic to meet President Roosevelt in August. The sailors in the *Repulse*, who were a little jealous of the *Prince of Wales* because their own vessel, though she had cruised in dangerous waters more than 50,000 miles during the war had only once come under bomb fire, called her half-admiringly 'The Glamour Ship,' and 'Churchill's Yacht.' They hoped that their own turn was now coming, and a notice pinned up in the *Repulse* read:

'To the Ship's Company, from the Captain.
We are off to look for trouble. I expect we shall find it.
We may run up against submarines or destroyers, aircraft or surface ships. . . .'

At about noon of the first day at sea, there came a sudden shout from the air-defence platform at the top of the main-mast.

'AIRCRAFT ON THE PORT BEAM!'

This second visitor turned out to be an R.A.F. Catalina flying boat and she signalled:

'Japanese making major landing north of Singora.'

It was exactly the kind of news that Admiral Phillips wanted to hear.

Later, a Japanese 'Nakajima Naka 93' plane appeared, though too far off for our guns to engage it. How much the pilot had spotted was a guess to all aboard.

The Japanese have, in fact, never made any official claim of a successful air reconnaissance, though they say that one of their submarines located and reported early that afternoon of 9th December, the whereabouts and movement of the British Fleet.

About the same time, Admiral Phillips debated whether or not to detach his destroyer escort (because of their 'low endurance') and send them back to Singapore, while he raced on to make a swift descent on Singora with the *Prince of Wales* and the *Repulse*. In this calculation, Phillips reckoned that the thick low clouds and the frequent squalls would deter hostile air action. He was also relying that the enemy planes which he encountered would not be equipped with anti-ship bombs or torpedoes, and that as he retired from his raid he would only have to deal with hastily summoned bombers from the Indo-China bases.

Then, as the evening skies cleared, more Japanese aircraft droned overhead. It was plain that they had now picked up our track, and they went on shadowing our ships until nightfall. Reluctantly, then, Admiral Phillips decided to abandon the Singora project, and gave orders to turn southward. Reporter O. D. Gallagher has told how his signal was greeted with groans in the wardroom of the *Repulse*.

'This d . . . d ship will never get into action! She's too b . . . lucky!'

In fact, the Japanese 22nd Air Flotilla, loading with bombs in Southern Indo-China for a raid on Singapore, had reloaded with torpedoes to deal with the British Fleet at sea, and had actually set off for a night attack. But the clouds clamped down again, compelling their return without ever making contact.

Aboard the **Prince of Wales**, at midnight, Admiral

Phillips received a signal from the Chief of Staff, Shore H.Q.

'Enemy reported landing at Kuantan.'

Kuantan is about 150 miles south of Kota Bharu, and would be on Phillips' way back to Singapore. Besides its value as an airfield, Kuantan was regarded as a key military position. It was about eight hours sailing from where the Fleet was at this time. The Admiral resolved to make for it. He would like to catch those Japanese somewhere by surprise!

But unaccountably, beyond a brief signal to Singapore indicating that the Fleet had turned back and was now headed there, Phillips sent off no further information. Tragically, for No. 453 (Fighter) Squadron was standing by in Singapore, specifically to provide escort for the Fleet if required. It could have been ordered up to Kuantan at any time, to be on call there.

Now trouble thickened. A second Japanese submarine had reported that night that the British Fleet were steering South and an air search patrol had been sent off, to be followed later by that formidable 22nd Air Flotilla striking force of 34 high-level bombers and 51 torpedo-bombers.

Soon after dawn on the morning of 10th December, bugles in the battleships blared 'ACTION STATIONS!' Enemy planes had been sighted—though they vanished again almost at once. A few minutes more, and from the decks of both the *Prince of Wales* and the *Repulse* our own aircraft were catapulted off to scout the coast and do anti-submarine patrol. The destroyer *Express* was also sent to reconnoitre.[1]

It was established that early on the previous night hostile ships had, indeed, been seen closing the shore near Kuantan. When our Beach Defences opened fire at them they had withdrawn. At daybreak, our Naval reconnaissance planes signalled back to the Fleet that no enemy remained around

[1]See *Despatches* of Air Chief Marshal Sir Robert Brooke-Popham, C.-in-C. Far East.

any longer, while the destroyer examining Kuantan harbour found there 'complete peace.'

Meantime, however, away to the East, the Fleet had observed a tug towing a number of barges, or junks—could they be landing-craft? Admiral Phillips decided to check.

By now, that Japanese air striking force which had some-how missed them in the early hours, and had since searched for them almost as far South as Singapore, was returning homeward. A Japanese plane, which had been shadowing the Fleet for about an hour, obviously warned them that their target lay right here. It was 11.15 a.m. when the first wave of high-level bombers approached, at about 10,000 feet, in tight line abreast. But before the initial main attack came in, Japanese bombers had swooped down on to the *Repulse*, drawing her very powerful ack-ack fire, then swung away again. It was an adroit diversion—and not the only one!

For bombs from the high-level planes crashed on to the air-catapult launching deck, penetrating the port hangar. Our own multiple pom-pom guns (the 'Chicago pianos') had been busy, and they shot down a Japanese plane about a thousand yards away. Then, as the cheers died, bugles sounded 'FIRE!' and smoke belched from the hangar.

Then, the second wave. This time it was the *Prince of Wales*' turn. She was struck, at the same moment, by a couple of torpedoes which were launched from planes which flew in (as at Singapore, following the opening blitz) in close forma-tion and at comparatively low level, for scattered clouds floated around at a thousand feet. Both port propellers of the *Prince of Wales* were put out of action, as well as her steering gear. She started to list heavily, and her speed fell from 25 to 15 knots. Soon, the *Prince of Wales* was little more than a floating wreck.

Next for treatment (ineffective, this time) was the *Repulse*, first by nine torpedo-bombers, from which she skilfully

turned away, and then from high level bombers, who likewise scored no hits.

Back to the *Prince of Wales!* More torpedo-bomb attacks, this time from starboardside. She, of course, could no longer avoid anything, and duly received another three hits. Toll exacted from the enemy: possibly, one more plane.

Repulse's second dose of torpedo bombing jammed her rudder and tore open her decks. But she shot down in flames a couple of her Japanese attackers, and 'everyone cheered with more abandon than any football crowd.' It was her crew's last war cry of defiance, for another torpedo now struck the ship, and she slowly heeled over and sank. Her multiple-guns went on firing to the last.

Then, for once—*Bushido!* As the British destroyers, *Vampire* and *Electra*, closed in to pick up the survivors in the water (there were no sharks around, the explosion had helped in that way), Japanese planes overhead signalled to the ships.

'We have completed our task. You may carry on.'

Nearly 800 out of 1,300 officers and men were saved.

It was 12.30 p.m. Quarter-of-an-hour later came the final bomb blast on the *Prince of Wales*, now a hulk capable of moving at only six knots. The Japs allowed the destroyer, *Express*, to run alongside her and take off the wounded. By 1.30 p.m. she, too, had gone beneath the waves. As the battleship sank, Buffalo fighters of 453 Squadron from Sembawang flew over the scene. They had been ordered to stand by at Sembawang airfield to provide air cover for the Fleet, if needed. Not until more than half-an-hour after the opening air attack on the Fleet was the first emergency signal radio-ed (from the *Repulse*). Another precious half-hour had passed before it reached operations room at Air Headquarters. When our fighters arrived, no Jap aircraft were in sight.

From the two British warships, 2,081 survivors (out of crews of 2,921) were rescued by our destroyers and taken safely to Singapore. Admiral Sir Tom Phillips, C.-in-C. Eastern Fleet, went down with his ships, as did their Captains, who were Capt. J. C. Leach (*Prince of Wales*) and Capt. W. G. Tennant (*Repulse*), though the latter officer was subsequently rescued. He would write one day in praise of the

'magnificent spirit of my officers and ship's company throughout this ordeal. Cases occurred of men having to be ordered to leave their guns to save themselves as the ship was actually turning over. . . .

When the ship had a 30 degree list to port, I looked

over the starboard side of the bridge and saw the commander and two or three hundred men collecting on the
starboard. I never saw the slightest sign of panic or ill-
discipline. I told them from the bridge how well they had
fought the ship and wished them good luck. The ship
hung for at least a minute-and-a-half to two minutes with
a list of about 60 or 70 degrees to port, then rolled over
at 12.33 p.m.'

Of the Jap victors, Capt. Tennant has recorded:

'The enemy attacks were without doubt magnificently
carried out and pressed well home. The high-level
bombers kept tight formation and appeared not to jink.
I observed only one torpedo-bomber who apparently had
cold feet and fired his torpedoes at a distance of at least
two miles from the ship.'[1]

And of the British survivors of this greatest naval disaster
there is the report from Flight-Lieut. T. A. Vigors, D.F.C., of
the R.A.A.F., the pilot of the first Buffalo to reach the scene
of it:

'It was obvious that the three destroyers were going to
take hours to pick up those hundreds of men clinging to
bits of wreckage and swimming round in the filthy, oily
water. Above all this, the threat of another bombing and
machine-gun attack was imminent. Every one of these
men must have realised that. Yet as I flew round, every
man waved and put up his thumb as I flew over him.
After an hour, lack of petrol forced me to leave, but
during that hour I had seen many men in dire danger
waving, cheering and joking, as if they were holiday-
makers at Brighton waving at a low-flying aircraft. It
shook me, for here was something above human
nature.'[2]

[1] *Despatches* of Vice-Admiral Sir Geoffrey Layton, K.C.B., D.S.O., C.-in-C.
Eastern Fleet, 17th December 1941.
[2] See above.

He was a blessed and lucky man, that pilot. The peoples of both the entire British Commonwealth and of the United States saw only the colossal size of the catastrophe, and there began to take shape a grim dread of its outcome. The effect of the loss of those two great ships upon the morale of all Services in Malaya was immediate, and immense.

'Unsinkable Dreadnought,' eh? And 'Impregnable Fortress,' too?

And how did the people in Britain feel? Winston Churchill has vividly described the way that the blow fell upon *him*.

The very night before this knock-out news broke in London, he had held a meeting in the Cabinet War Room at No. 10 Downing Street, to review the naval position. As he says, we had lost the command of every ocean except the Atlantic—and Australia, New Zealand and all the vital islands in their area were now wide open to invasion. One key weapon was left in our hands, that pair of great capital warships, the *Prince of Wales* and the *Repulse*.

As long as their whereabouts were unknown to the enemy, they represented a real menace to all his naval plans. It was agreed that they should vanish amid the many islands of Malaya. It was Churchill's own opinion that they should then sail across the Pacific Ocean to join the remnants of the American Fleet which had survived the Pearl Harbour calamity. As he has written:

> 'It would be a proud gesture at this moment, and would knit the English-speaking world together. We had already cordially agreed to the American Navy Department withdrawing their capital ships from the Atlantic. Thus in a few months there might be a fleet in being on the west coast of America capable of fighting a decisive sea battle if need be. The existence of such a fleet and of such a fact would be the best possible shield to our brothers in Australasia.'

'We were all much attracted by this line of thought. But

---

[1]*The Second World War* Vol. III by Winston S. Churchill.

Australian reinforcements disembark at Singapore

'Scorched earth policy.' Indian Army sappers preparing to mine a bridge near Kuala Lumpur

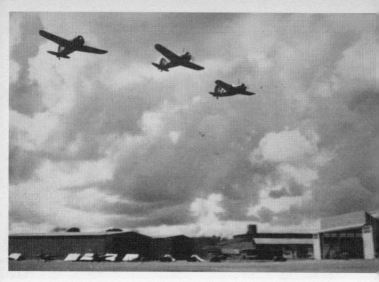

Brewster Buffalo fighter planes flying in to their Malayan airfield

Air Vice-Marshal C. W. H. Pulford greets men of the Dutch Air Force

as the hour was late we decided to sleep on it, and settle the next morning what to do with the *Prince of Wales* and the *Repulse*.'

'Within a couple of hours they were at the bottom of the sea.'[1]

Next morning, the telephone at Churchill's bedside rang. It was a call from the First Sea Lord. With a slight cough and gulp, he began:

'Prime Minister, I have to report to you that the *Prince of Wales* and the *Repulse* have both been sunk by the Japanese —we think by aircraft. Tom Phillips is drowned.'

'Are you sure it's true?'

'There is no doubt at all.'

Churchill put down the telephone. He was glad to be alone.

'In all the war,' he wrote, 'I never received a more direct shock . . . As I turned over and twisted in bed the full horror of the news sank in upon me. There were no British or American capital ships in the Indian Ocean or the Pacific except the American survivors of Pearl Harbour, who were hastening back to California. Over all this vast expanse of waters Japan was supreme, and we everywhere were weak and naked.'[2]

Before noon, Churchill had told the brief news of this giant disaster to an astounded and hushed House of Commons.

Next day, he made a full review of the entire war situation, as it now stood.

Again, a grim silence fell.

[1]*Ibid.*
[2]*Ibid.*

CHAPTER FIVE

SOUTH OF THE BORDER

Mᴏʀᴇ immediate misfortune had already fallen on the British Air Defence of Malaya.

On 9th December, Air Vice-Marshal Pulford, Air Officer Commanding Far East, had ordered up from Singapore half-a-dozen Blenheims of his slender bomber force for an attack on Singora, the base in Southern Siam which had been carefully prepared by the Japanese for months before they opened war in South-East Asia.

But with the cancellation of Operation MATADOR, our planes had been withdrawn from the advanced airfield at Alor Star, in the State of Kedah, to Butterworth, in Province Wellesley. It was at this latter point that fighter escort were to have joined our bombers but, as it happened, they could not be spared. So, the Blenheims flew on alone. They ran into 30 enemy fighters (as well as heavy ack-ack fire from Singora airfield), and though they took some toll of the aircraft which were grounded there, they lost half of their own number.

A second British air raid, planned to fly from Butterworth at 5 o'clock the same evening, never even got away from the ground. For as our planes lined up for their take-off, down from on high poured a hail of Japanese bombs, followed by a devastating machine-gun scorching fire at low level. Every Blenheim, except one, was destroyed or damaged on the runway.

The survivor had got off just as the first enemy attack came in, and after circling around above the blazing airfield until it was obvious that no other British plane was going to join him, the pilot, Squadron Leader A. S. K. Scarf, flew away to Singora on his own. There, in the face of fierce Japanese fighter attack and ack-ack bombardment, he pressed home his attack. He was mortally wounded, and reckoning that he would not live long enough to make the return flight to Butterworth, he safely crash-landed his Blenheim at Alor Star without hurt to his crew. Rushed to hospital, Scarf died within the hour that night. This valiant pilot was awarded a posthumous Victoria Cross.

Now the enemy had seized the skies of North Malaya. By dawn, 10th December, the total of R.A.F. planes still operative there had fallen from above a hundred to half that number. After only two days' battle, the Japanese air strength outstripped the British by ten to one. Our ground defences were lacking enough ack-ack guns, and even an effective air raid warning system, so that over and over again our planes were caught while refuelling or reloading, and were blotted out where they stood.

So heavy were the casualties that already, on 9th December, Air Vice-Marshal Pulford had decided to withdraw most of his aircraft even from Kuantan, which as the most northerly seaport in the State of Pahang is more than half-way down the East coast of Malaya. Before the evacuation order could be carried out the Japanese air raiders were on the scene, bombing and machine-gunning, and without being hindered by a single piece of ack-ack artillery. They disposed of another eight British planes. Thereafter, Kuantan was used by the R.A.F. only as an advanced landing ground.

That same night of 9th December, had come air reports of steamships towing barges and assault craft towards the mouth of Kuantan River. The alarm was swiftly passed to III Corps, and throughout the hours of darkness the 2/18th Royal Garhwal Rifles manned the beach defences, while six Vildebeeste and three Hudson planes scoured the seas. Their total 'bag' was three small ships, which they bombed (with rather doubtful results).

Next morning, no trace of these targets was to be found, though it seems that the beaches had actually been fired on. It may have been a light reconnaissance by the enemy to test the strength of these defences, for some days later several boats and small junks were found further down the coast, containing some Japanese equipment. More probably, it was part of the enemy's general design (an extremely successful one!) to stir up alarm throughout the entire peninsula of Malaya.

Be this as it may, its mark upon the War in South-East Asia is sure. Remember, it was the reports of a Japanese landing at Kuantan which had led Admiral Sir Tom Phillips, with his *Prince of Wales* and *Repulse* towards that ill-fated shore.

And it was because the R.A.F. fighter squadrons had been withdrawn from Kuantan airfield only the previous day that, when the Force Z Fleet of those great battleships and their attendant destroyers were attacked by the Japanese bombers, there followed the failure to provide them with air cover in time to save them.

Now came fresh warp-and-woof in the pattern of defeat. Because it was impossible to keep our outnumbered Air Force based on the forward airfields in Northern Malaya, we had to withdraw them next from Butterworth, in Province Wellesley, on the mainland opposite Penang Island. The effect of these repeated evacuations was not a happy one, either on the Royal Air Force or the Royal Australian Air Force squadrons who had to take part in them. Wrote Air Vice-Marshal Sir Paul Maltby, later Assistant Air Officer Commanding, Far East, in his despatches:[1]

'Some of the personnel of No. 21 (F) Squadron R.A.A.F. and No. 27 (NF) Squadron R.A.F. both of which had

[1]*Despatch* by Air Vice-Marshal Sir Paul Maltby on air operations during the campaign in Malaya and the Netherlands East Indies from 8th December 1941 to 12th March 1942. (*Supplement to London Gazette* of 20/2/48, No. 38216.)

already been driven out of Sungei Patani, did not behave
at all steadily.'

Incidentally, these airfield evacuations were rarely well
carried out.

Thus, both at Sungei Patani and at Kuantan large stocks
of petrol, oil and stores were left to the enemy. It is true
that in some air stations there were not even explosives
available to blow up the abandoned material. In other
places, perhaps it was just as well that it was 'Operation Guy
Fawkes' itself which had to be abandoned.

For the timing of it had to be so precisely adjusted. If you
left it too late, then the enemy would collect the booty intact.
But if you did it too soon, then the crash of the explosions,
the flash of fire and the pall of smoke rising in the rear of the
troops who were fighting off the enemy could cause—and
more than once *did* cause—alarm, and even panic. Finally,
therefore, the order went forth that no fires were to be started.
Instead, petrol and oil were to be run to waste; buildings
were to be smashed-up only, and any demolitions requiring
the use of explosives were to be left to the sappers.

Some discreditable incidents marred parts of this 'Operation Clear-out'. There were tales of gun hold-ups of private
cars (and even of public omnibuses) by panic-stricken
Servicemen, desperate to get away at all costs. There was
some looting, too, and even shooting.

Another problem which arose, of course, was the one
affecting the civilian population who were staying on in this
militarily abandoned land. Orders arrived from the War
Cabinet in London prescribing an unrestricted 'Scorched
Earth' policy, i.e. the destruction of railways, bridges, harbours, electricity stations, power and lighting plants, reservoirs, food storehouses, etc., in order to deny them to the
enemy.

This was not too easy a plan to carry out, either, in
somebody else's homeland—and especially in the face of the
current cunning Japanese propaganda appeal of '*Asia for the*

Asiatics!' After exchanges between Singapore and London, the order was curtailed so as not to apply to foodstuffs already issued to the civilian population, to water supplies, or power plants.

On 10th December, 80 Japanese bombers swooped in and strafed Penang. Now, though this island was officially referred to as 'Fortress Penang,'[1] it possessed no real anti-aircraft defences (the guns long-promised from Britain had not even yet arrived) and only a few bomb shelters. The casualties ran into thousands.

Our own aircraft, Brewster Buffalo fighters and Blenheim and Vickers-Vildebeeste bombers, now withdrawn southward to Ipoh in the middle of the State of Perak, besides being utterly outnumbered were also quite outmatched by the more modern Japanese Navy 96 fighters, their twin-engined Navy 96 and Army 97 bombers, and their Junker 87 N dive-bombers.

This same day of 10th December, a fresh Japanese landing came in from the sea at Besut, 30 miles south of Kota Bharu on the East coast and near the large new airfield at Gong Kedah. Lacking any air reconnaissance to check the strength of this invasion, Brigadier Key, Commander of the 'Kelantan Force,' decided to abandon both the Gong Kedah airfield and the one at Machang, which is further inland. Neither of them was now any longer required by our own Air Force, and to hold on to them would be to risk having the enemy cut across the only road and railway which led to the South. Time was too short for Brigadier Key even to complete his plans to blow up the airfield runways.

There began a 12-day fighting retreat by 'Kelantan Force' down the jungle mountain railway from Kuala Krai to Kuala Lipis, in the neighbouring State of Pahang. Indeed, it developed into a struggle as to which side should do most damage to the railway, by destroying its fine bridges spanning the ravines. Could the British rearguard blow each bridge and escape,—before the Japanese could follow in their track?

[1]cf. 'Fortress Singapore!' Author's note.

Or could the Japanese slip around the main British force, get ahead of their advance guard—and blow the bridge before they could reach it, thus trapping them?

The rearguard, commanded by Lieutenant-Colonel McKellan (it was known as 'Macforce' and included troops of the Pahang Volunteers and the Malay Regiment), faithfully did its duty. Bombed by the Japanese Air Force all along the narrow track of this 140 miles of single railway line which stretches down the mountain backbone of Malaya, and without either cover from our own weakened Air Force or retaliation by them upon the pursuing enemy, Brigadier Key succeeded in extricating the greater part of his troops, thus saving them for the battle now developing on the West Coast, where every man was desperately needed.

Here, the other two prongs of the Japanese Invasion Fork were stabbing down southward into Malaya. Along the railway and the roads nearest to the sea went two regiments of the Japs' Fifth Division, supported by tanks and field gun batteries, with orders to annihilate the British forces still massed at Jitra, where there is a junction of two roads from Siam. Down that mountain road which leads from The Ledge in Siam, across the frontier to Kroh in Malaya, sped another regiment of the Fifth Division, likewise strongly reinforced with both armour and artillery. The particular object of this exercise was to break through to the right and cut off any British forces fighting in the State of Kedeh, Penang or North Perak.

The British position at Jitra was never a good one. Its defences had not been completed when the War in the Far East broke out. Barbed-wire lines had to be erected and anti-tank mines laid—while all the time in these December days a steady downpour of rain flooded the shallow trenches and gun pits. Many of the field telephone cables hurriedly laid across the waterlogged ground failed to work.

Two brigades of Major-General Murray-Lyon's 11th Indian Division held the front line. On the right, were the 15th Indian Brigade, composed of 1st Leicestershires, the

1/14th Punjab Regiment and the 2/9th Jats; on the left, were the 6th Indian Brigade, composed of the East Surreys, the 1/8th Punjab Regt. and the 2/16th Punjab Regt. Batteries from the 155th Field Regiment, the 22nd Mountain Regiment and the 80th Anti-Tank Regiment provided the artillery support. In reserve, were the 28th Indian Brigade.

It was a very wide front, stretching across both roads and the railway, of course, and far beyond on either side, from the jungle-clad hills on the right *via* flooded rice fields and a rubber estate to a tidal mangrove swamp on the left. Altogether, perhaps 14 miles.

Shortly after dawn of 10th December, the Japanese advance guard followed back over the frontier the Punjabi force which had crossed it to destroy the bridges beyond (Chapter Three). It was not until the following day that the two sides became locked in battle, and then a Japanese mechanised force swept down the road and threw into wild confusion a column of Punjabis as they moved up to the line. The Japanese also took heavy toll of a Gurkha unit. It was the first time that most of these Indian troops had ever set eyes on a tank.

That night, further trouble piled upon the Jitra garrison as the outpost troops fell back towards the main position. The British officer responsible for the demolition of a road bridge over a stream blew it as our men (whom he mistook for the enemy) approached it. We lost a dozen guns on the far side. Throughout the hours of darkness a muddled battle continued, in which the Japanese tanks and carriers several times broke into our front but were later thrown out. On one of these occasions, as the Punjabis drove the enemy off they came under heavy fire themselves from a nearby Jat unit of their own side.

Next morning, to add to his anxieties at Jitra, Major-General Murray-Lyon learnt that 'Krohcol,' the force which had fought the battle for The Ledge, was being forced to retreat. Now this could constitute a real threat to his own line of communications—and his 11th Indian Division was the only one with which Northern Malaya could be defended. He asked for permission to retire from Jitra to a position he had already selected about 30 miles southward, at Gurun. This was a natural stronghold, though it had not yet been put into a state of active defence.

When Murray-Lyon's request came through to III Corps Headquarters, Lieutenant-General Heath, the Corps Commander, had gone to Singapore to consult Lieutenant-General Percival, General Officer Commanding Malaya, about the grave developments on the East Coast. The request was therefore telephoned direct to Percival's own Headquarters.

He firmly refused it.

Quite apart from his objections to Murray-Lyon's plan on tactical grounds, Percival feared that such an early and such a long retreat would have a demoralising effect both on the troops and on the civilian population. This opinion was endorsed by the Far East War Council in Singapore that same morning and Murray-Lyon was told that, pending further orders, the battle must be fought out at Jitra.

All that day it raged. By about 1.0 p.m. the Japanese had driven a deep wedge into the centre of 15th Indian Brigade's position on the right flank. A flood of wild rumours nearly set off a panic in some sections, especially when the enemy artillery was able to bring under close-range fire the only bridge across the unfordable River Bata, which lay in the British rear.

By evening, so dangerously had the situation deteriorated that at 7.30 p.m., Murray-Lyon again sought leave to fall back to the position at Gurun. Since III Corps Commander had not yet been able to fly back to his Headquarters, the message was once more relayed direct to Malaya Command H.Q. This time, General Percival agreed that Murray-Lyon should be given discretion to withdraw from Jitra. His task now, he was told, was to try and hold North Kedah and the best tactics would probably be to block up the enemy tanks on good natural obstacles, and to dispose his forces so as to obtain real depth on the two parallel North-South roads which traversed the rice-growing area, and thus get greater scope for his artillery.

At 10 p.m. Murray-Lyon issued orders for the 11th Indian Division to withdraw to the South bank of the River Kedah at Alor Star, beginning at midnight.

> 'This withdrawal' writes General Percival, 'would have been difficult under the most favourable conditions. With the troops tired, units mixed as the result of the fighting, communications broken and the night dark, it was inevitable that orders should be delayed and that in some cases they should never reach the addressees. This is what in fact occurred. Some units and sub-units withdrew without incident. Others, finding themselves unable to use the only road, had to make their way as best they could across country. On the left flank, there were no roads, so some parties reached the coast and, taking boats, rejoined farther south. Some, again, were still in position the following morning. The fact is that the withdrawal, necessary as it may have been, was too fast and too complicated for disorganised and exhausted troops, whose disorganisation and exhaustion it only increased.'[1]

The retreat by night down a single, narrow jungle road, and in an appalling storm, was a near-calamity. It might have been an utter one but for another resolute rearguard action.

At midnight, on December 12/13th, the Japanese made a determined effort to rush that only bridge over the River Bata. They were violently repulsed by the 2/2nd Gurkha Rifles. Two hours later, the bridge was blown and the battalion withdrew through a rearguard formed by 2/9th Gurkha Rifles, who fought another fierce engagement before, at 4.30 a.m., themselves retiring. Then, until the sun had passed high noon, all contact with the pursuing enemy was broken.

It had, indeed, been a devastating experience. The British

[1]'*The War in Malaya*' by Lieutenant General A. E. Percival. See above.

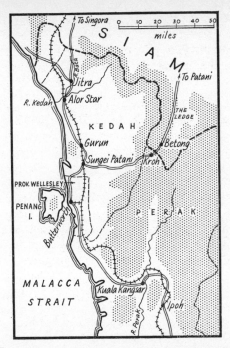

casualties and their loss of guns, ammunition, equipment and transport were heavy. The early yielding of a prepared defensive position at a key point was a grave strategical setback. Even graver, was the slumping of morale among the survivors—and its still more widespread effect upon units not yet in contact with the enemy. Gravest of all, was the fact that this shattering defeat had been inflicted on a British Indian Division by a Japanese advance guard roughly equal in strength to only two battalions (i.e. less than a quarter), supported by a squadron of tanks.

What was the cause of it?

No doubt the abandonment of Operation MATADOR played its considerable part in the tragedy. Training for a bold advance into Siam to secure Singora and Patani before the invading Japanese could seize these vital bridgeheads had used up precious time which could otherwise have been devoted to strengthening the defence works of the Jitra position —and, indeed, practising the necessary defence tactics.

More fatal still, was the psychological setback inflicted on fighting men who were told, first, to expect to conduct warfare from strongly fortified lines, then warned to be ready to march forward overnight against the enemy, then told to stand still and wait, and then ordered to man the defences— which, by this time, were knee deep in mire and rainwater. Much of the confusion was due to lack of effective staff co-ordination between local commands.

Add to these factors, the constant drain upon all units in the Indian Army throughout 1940-1 for trained men to serve in the Middle East and Mediterranean theatres of war, and the inevitable allocation to those actively operational areas of the equipment, weapons and machinery which all personnel must be provided with if they are to master their craft as soldiers.

Yes, and set against the part-training of these recently raised and still utterly inexperienced British Indian Army units the very thoroughly schooled and firmly (even brutally) disciplined Imperial Guards of Nippon! Very many of these were not only veterans of the previous years of Japan's wars against China, but had been specifically instructed in jungle fighting and seaborne assault landing for this very war.

Was it possible that the still almost raw recruits who made up such a substantial bulk of the defenders of Malaya could learn in overnight fighting there the lessons of war, in time to meet their tough and seasoned enemy?

As night fell on 12th December, the Japanese were speeding down the Patani-Kroh road towards its junction with the Jitra-Sungei Patani road. If they could get there before the 11th Indian Division had extricated itself from North Kedah, then the sole garrison of all North Malaya would be captive.

CHAPTER SIX

LOSS OF NORTH MALAYA

Dawn of 13th December brought a new Day of Confusion.

As the stragglers from the mixed-up battle of Jitra made their way South across the Kedah River, in groups or individually, Japanese snipers disguised in Malayan dress mingled with them, then broke away into the jungle on either side of the road to pick themselves a cover from which they could carry on their killing. Not difficult to do in that dense undergrowth of fern, thorn, thicket and creepers.

Two incidents illustrate the chaos which reigned.

That morning, as General Murray-Lyon, the Divisional Commander, himself stood on the road bridge South of Alor Star, watching the rearguards closing in, three motor cyclists came weaving in and out of a convoy of army trucks. As he sped past the General, the first one waved and laughed at him.

'My God!' cried Murray-Lyon. 'That's a Jap!'

He tore his revolver from his holster, and with the officers who were accompanying him, dealt with the other two motor cyclists. But the first one was already far down the road.

Now, Murray-Lyon gave the order to blow both the road and the railway bridges. But the explosive charges had been hastily laid, and the railway bridge merely sagged and did not break. On the far side of the river stood an armoured train of ours, which was going to be wrecked there and abandoned.

It was now decided to use it, for the last time, to complete the demolition of the bridge.

The driver steamed up the engine, pulled the whistle, slipped the brake, and leapt from the footplate as the train moved towards the bridge. The whistle jammed, and shrieking above the roar of the engine and the rumble of the trucks and the rattle of rifle-fire from the advancing enemy, the load of armour rolled on to the bending bridge.

Bending, but still not breaking! And when the train reached the mid-stream point where the rails had been severed, it simply leapt over the crack and trundled on across to the southern bank of the river and disappeared down the jungle track with its crew sprinting after it. The bridge had to be blown after all.

It was done only just in time. For the Japanese advance guard had now arrived on the riverline, and that afternoon they actually forced their way across and gained a foothold on the South bank, though a counter-attack by the 2/9th Gurkha Rifles threw them back beyond the river.

But our troops were in no form to resist a full scale attack; indeed, many of them had never known a rest since the fighting began five days ago. So Murray-Lyon ordered the retreat to be resumed. That night, in inky darkness and soaking rain and along a road jammed with trucks, the soldiers squelched their way through sludge towards the next stop.

This was around a cross-roads near Gurun, 20 miles South. The British position, which lay astride the main road and the railway on rubber estates between the lower slopes of the 4,000 ft. Kedah Peak on the West and the flat, thick-forested land on the East, had been reconnoitered and mapped-out. But though it had been actually selected as a defence site before the outbreak of war, no work whatever had been done to prepare it. Since then, during the past week, orders had indeed been issued to assemble a large civilian labour force under military supervision and get on with the job. But, says General Percival,

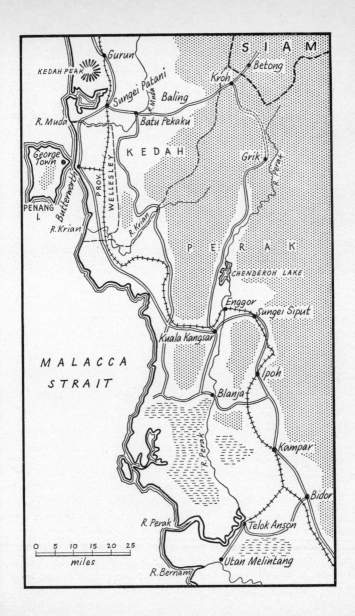

'Whether they had ever assembled and dispersed, or never assembled at all, I cannot say as reports on this point are conflicting.'[1]

In fact, very few actually did arrive on the scene. For this, some considerable responsibility must rest upon the War Office in London, which had fixed a rate of pay for labour far below that which ruled in civilian jobs.[2]

So, the tired fighting men of the 11th Indian Division would have to dig their own trenches and gun pits. (That is to say that they would have had to dig them, if time had permitted.) It did not!

The rearguard had barely passed through our front lines, about 2 p.m. when Japanese bombers appeared.

Under their covering fire about a dozen lorries, supported by three tanks, rushed down the main road and unloaded several hundred infantrymen. The tanks were a particular surprise, for it had been reckoned that the destruction of the bridges would hold them up for several days. Their arrival was just one more proof that the enemy had thoroughly planned this campaign, and supplied himself with the vital engineering equipment for it.

The swift attack of the Japanese gave them a wedge into the British front near the cross-roads. This sector was manned by some recent members of 'Laycol,' the 1/8th Punjab Regiment, of the 6th Indian Brigade, who had been severely battered during the retreat. The situation was saved by Brigadier Lay, who launched a vigorous counter-attack, leading it himself in person.

The Japanese, however, held on to the cross-roads and late that night, as Lay made ready for another assault at dawn, they struck first. Opening with a fierce mortar bombardment,

---

[1] In his book, '*The War in Malaya*' (see above).
[2] An argument drooled on for weeks in the War Council at Singapore over the recruitment of civil labour. Whitehall would not sanction the payment of more attractive wages than local industry was offering, and the Director-General of Civil Defence opposed any real measure of compulsion, until nearly the end of January 1942, when better wages and working conditions were also at last settled.

they broke through the Punjabi lines, stormed into the Headquarters, both of the neighbouring 2nd East Surrey Regiment
and of the 6th Brigade itself, killing almost the entire staffs.
Brigadier Lay himself escaped only because he had just gone
off to another part of the front.

It was at this point of midnight mix-up and alarm that
the commander of the Punjabis, believing that the neighbouring units on his right flank had been wiped out, decided to
withdraw his own surviving troops westward and seek to
rejoin the rest of the Division later by marching down the
coastal road.

His action left the main road to the South wide open but,
strangely, for once, the enemy did not press on. When, at
daybreak, Murray-Lyon surveyed the battlefield, he realised
the perilous position of his 28th Brigade on the East of the
main road and railway, and immediately ordered them to
retire beyond Gurun. As noon came, he made the further decision to continue his retreat to the Muda River, which forms
the boundary between the State of Kedah and Province
Wellesley. It meant another 20 miles of tramping for his
battle-worn men.

At least, however, one ominous threat to the 11th Division
was thereby removed. This came from the drive of the *other*
Japanese prong down the Kroh road, and it might well have
resulted in the enemy slashing the sole British line of retreat
at Sungei Patani, where the two highways meet. Down this
Kroh road, therefore, plodded the force known as 'Krohcol.'

But as it passed through the village of Kroh, another
(though a remoter) danger developed. This was that the
enemy, besides pressing after the 'Krohcol' rearguards to
Sungei Patani, would switch a force along the road that runs
due South via Grik to the town of Kuala Kangsar, which is
another junction on the main West Coast highway. Much of
this Kroh-Kuala Kangsar route was merely a rough, un-
metalled mountain track, but if the Japanese could get along
it to Kuala Kangsar ahead of us they would trap the
11th Indian Division totally, and 'Krohcol,' too.

To Grik, therefore, to block this path General Sir Lewis Heath, commanding III Indian Corps, despatched a company of the 2nd Argyll and Sutherland Highlanders, supported by some armoured cars of the Federated Malay States Volunteers. The rest of the battalion moved up to Baling, on the Kroh-Sungei Patani road.

The major question now arose: *What was to be done about the Island of Penang?*

We have seen this place, also, described officially as a 'fortress'—and exposed subsequently as being utterly nothing of the sort. Its military value lay in its port facilities, its substantial stocks of ammunition and stores, and the fact that it was the terminus of the ocean cables which connected Malaya with India and Ceylon.

But the civil airport on the island was too small for R.A.F. operations, and the airfield on the mainland at Butterworth, in Province Wellesley, was not much more use. The only fighter defence which Penang ever had was provided on one day alone by a squadron of Buffaloes (453 F) which arrived on 13th December from Singapore.

Of the fixed defences which had been approved for this 'fortress,' only two six-inch batteries with their searchlights had been installed, and NONE of the anti-aircraft defence material had arrived when the first two air raids took place on 11th and 12th December, on Georgetown, the principal commercial and residential community of Penang Island.

As crowds thronged the streets to watch the aircraft, the Japanese planes swooped down, bombing and machine-gunning. They took a toll of about 2,000 killed and wounded of the gaping, gasping population, and set the town afire. The corpses cluttered the streets, for most of the police and the entire labour force had now deserted. A sickening stench arose.

Well, was Penang Island to be held?

The island is about 150 square miles in area, and its garrison at the time of the retreat from North Malaya mustered totally about the strength of two weak battalions, half of which were regular soldiers and the rest partly-trained members of the Straits Settlements Volunteer Force.

It had been Percival's original intention to reinforce Penang with two more infantry battalions and supporting troops, and then defend it to the death.

Already, on 12th December, it was decided between the Fortress Commander (Brigadier Lyon) and the Resident Counsellor (Mr Forbes) to evacuate the next night all European woman and children and as many of the sick and wounded as could be moved from the Military Hospital. It was not thought possible to shift all the Asian civilians, because of the lack of enough transport (perhaps an inevitable, but as we shall see, an unfortunate decision).

On 13th December, there arrived in Penang about 50 British bluejackets, survivors from the *Prince of Wales* and *The Repulse*, sent thither to operate the ferries, for the native crews of these had vanished, too. That night, the hospital evacuation was carried out as planned.

Next morning, 14th December, at a meeting of the Far East War Council, General Percival raised the entire problem of Penang. There was no question now of committing more troops to the defence of the island, for every available man was needed for the fighting on the mainland if the Japanese advance was to be stemmed. If it could not be, then Penang was lost anyway.

The value of its anchorage to the Navy had already gone. General Heath, Commanding III Corps, was therefore given discretion to act as he deemed fit in withdrawing the garrison and as many essential military stores as possible. On 15th December, he issued the necessary orders to clear the island the following night. The Civil Authorities were already warning that an outbreak of cholera and typhoid was at hand.

There was little time left to destroy all the ammunition stocks, the oil and petrol stores, the equipment, and to deny the enemy the use of the machinery and the facilities of a great port. Something was done, including the wrecking of the power station, though much was left undone (perhaps because certain leading persons in charge so swiftly evacuated themselves) and at least two major mishaps marred this 'Operation Sabotage' at Penang.

The **first** was the failure to blow up the building and radio plant of the British Malayan Broadcasting Corporation, which within a week was pouring out a torrent of violent anti-British propaganda. The **second** was the failure to sail away or to scuttle all the small ships, barges and junks which were tied up in the harbour. These included a couple of dozen self-propelled craft, and they proved to be of infinite use to the Japanese in the next phase of seaborne operations along the West coast of Malaya. Later, a British destroyer made a daring night voyage to mine the southern channel leading from the harbour, but did not succeed, either.

The decision to restrict the civilian evacuation of Penang Island to Europeans was much criticised at the time, both in Malaya and elsewhere—and the Jap-controlled Penang Broadcasting Station naturally did not omit to make full exploitation of it.

But with only four ferry boats and those scratch R.N. ferry service crews, hardly more was possible on the two nights of the operation. And even if thousands of Asian citizens had crossed over to the mainland, it would still have been quite impossible during a desperate retreat to provide enough transport to carry them on to Singapore. Nor, in fact, was the accommodation available for them there. Probably, they were better off in Penang. About 500 Asian members of the Straits Settlements Volunteer Force, with their arms and equipment, chose to stay on the island with their families.

(They at least escaped the experience of the civilian refugees from Perak State, who were ordered South by the military. Arriving in a packed train at Kuala Lumpur, they were met by an officer with a telegram from Sir Shenton Thomas, Governor of the Straits Settlements, saying that no more people could come to crowded Singapore. They were herded back into the train and were taken as far North as the

frontier of Perak State—where the military sent them off
again to Kuala Lumpur.)

With Penang abandoned, there was no longer any sound
military reason for 11th Division to hang on to the line of the
Muda River—especially since the Japanese were pressing
down both the roads from Kroh and were threatening to
outflank 11th Division, if not actually block their line of
retreat.

General Percival tells a story of one of the tricks which the
enemy played in his efforts to seize a bridge at Batu Pekaku.
It had been partly demolished, and was guarded by a Punjabi
sentry. A man in civilian clothes, pretending to be a local
British planter, appeared at the far end and asked leave to
come across. Covering him with his tommy gun, the sentry
beckoned him over. As the stranger came close, he made a
sudden leap at the Punjabi and grappled with him. A lucky
blow from the soldier, and a second later the intruder lay
dead at his feet. He was a German, serving with the Japanese.
Dressed in native clothes, his allies were double-marching at
that moment towards the bridgehead. They got an unexpected
reception.

General Heath now made ready to retire a further lap, this
time to Krian River, 30 miles away towards the key point of
roads at Kuala Kangsar. The intervening country is fairly flat
and open, and therefore suitable for tank warfare, in which
the invaders could command an overwhelming superiority.
So Heath had sound reasons for getting his foot-borne (and
grimly foot-sore) men behind this next river barrier, with
its extensive thorned swamps, as soon as possible. Fighting a
series of spirited rearguard actions, the 11th Division trod
their way towards the Krian, and by dawn of 18th December
the entire force had crossed to the southern bank.

Surely, at last, there could be a halt and a brief browse for
the dog-tired troops?

No! there was still—and even more than ever—the threat
of that other thrust of the invaders down the mountain road
from Grik to Kuala Kangsar. As we know now, from

Japanese official sources which have been made available since the war, it was a major part of their strategy to chop the British line of communication precisely at this point.

Holding up the enemy was the small force of the 2nd Argyll and Sutherland Highlanders. On 19th December, they were reinforced by the rest of their battalion and a company of the 5/2nd Punjabis. It was not too soon, for the very next day they had to contain both frontal assaults on the road and attempted flanking attacks by raft down the Perak River which at this point runs closely parallel to it.

The problem facing General Percival in these tough mid-December days was, indeed, a complex one.

His prime duty, insistently re-affirmed by the War Cabinet in London, was to defend Singapore Naval Base.

To do this, Percival had to hold the enemy as far North on the mainland of Malaya as possible. For if the Japanese could gain the use of the airfields within near range of Singapore, then they could mount mass-bombing onslaughts on the Island, the City, and the Naval Harbour—whenever they chose—and they could also give close fighter support to their own bombers.

Still more, if they commanded the sea approaches to Singapore, then the Japanese could prevent the arrival of any ships and the disembarkation of any troops or fighter aircraft reinforcement. (For since the early capture of the airfield at Victoria Point, at the southernmost extremity of Burma, the enemy had made it impossible for us to fly short-range planes in to Malaya from India and Burma; they had to be crated in cargo vessels and unloaded on the quays, or else flown in from carriers off-shore).

But, always, a second thought gnawed at Percival's mind.

If he massed his strength too far northward—and the Japs, with their command of the sea, invaded to the southward, could they be held there?

For the moment (the morning of 18th December), there was no Jap pressure on the line of the Krian River—a cause for some anxiety and suspicion on the British side.

Just what was the enemy up to now? Carrying out some far outflanking march through the mountain jungle? Or a seaborne operation designed to land a force at a river mouth well in our rear?

From Singapore, General Percival had already had a word by telephone with General Heath, commanding III Corps, and meeting now about noon this morning at Ipoh, 30 miles south of Kuala Kangsar, they agreed that it would be tactically wise to withdraw all our troops behind the Perak River.

As the map shows[1], for many a mile further the Perak River runs due South, i.e. parallel with the line of our main road and rail communications. However, since steep, wooded mountain ranges lie between the river and the coast, it was unlikely that the enemy could strike across our retreat unless he could force his way through either of two defiles. The first of these ran out from Kuala Kangsar itself, the key junction of roads from Grik and from Penang. The second was at Blanja, 20 miles further down the Perak River, where a pontoon bridge spanned it. The British plan was to hold the invaders West of the river as long as possible.

Of course, they had to be contained to the northward, too. But within the next day or so, they had pushed the Argylls and the Punjabis of the 12th Indian Brigade down the Grik road as far as the shores of Chenderoh Lake. This is a couple of miles wide and about five miles long; it obviously offered the well-equipped attacking force the opportunity to exploit their advantages of equipment, and this they did in a series of day and night raft-borne operations.

The danger, again, was that not only would they slip in behind the Argylls and the Punjabis and isolate them before they could retire down the road to Kuala Kangsar. It was that they would cross the lake in strength, land on the South-eastern shore, and shove along parallel to the road over the intervening swamp lands until they reached both the railway bridge at Enggor and the huge newly-built road bridge at

[1]See page 79.

Iskandar, which link Kuala Kangsar itself with the next town on our line of retreat, Sungei Siput. The 4/19th Hyderabad Regiment, which had just fallen back from the Kelantan Front, were ordered to cover this approach, and splendidly they did it.

Already, the 28th Indian Brigade, who had been our flank guard on the West Coast, were nearing Kuala Kangsar. They had broken all the bridges behind them, and done their damndest to flood the oozy, flat shorelands by blowing-up the water-pipes.

But the water drains down to the sea, and the river levels sink with the tide, so that at certain hours you can wade across places where once a bridge had been.

The 28th Brigade fell back slowly enough to allow the 12th Brigade to evacuate Kuala Kangsar in good order, cross the Iskandar Bridge (destroying it, along with Enggor Bridge), and retire towards Sungei Siput on the main road and railway track towards Ipoh. The other task of the 28th Brigade was to garrison the second entrance into the Perak Valley (and across Perak River) at Blanja. This they also did, sinking the pontoon bridge there around midnight, 23/24th December.

During these days and nights of desperate fighting, some drastic changes had been made necessary in the set-up of the 11th Division, both in unit formations and in their command.

Thus, the 12th Brigade was now brought into the Division, and due to the heavy casualties suffered both by the 6th and the 15th Brigades, it was decided to merge them, henceforth to be known as the 6/15th Brigade. Battalions, too, got 'married,' like the pair from the 16th Punjab Regiment, and the two British battalions from the Leicesters and the East Surreys (who were registered as the 'British Battalion'). It says a lot for the true comradely spirit of this still so little-known Army of Malaya that these forced unions worked out so well in the battles yet to be fought.

In Brigade leadership there was a certain amount of switching, due to the appointment of Brigadier Paris, of the 12th

Indian Brigade, to succeed Maj.-Gen. Murray-Lyon as Commander of the 11th Division. Still more important, were the changes which took place at the same time on the topmost level.

Here, Lieut.-General Sir Henry Pownall had arrived in Singapore, on 23rd December, to relieve Air Chief Marshal Sir Robert Brooke-Popham as Commander-in-Chief, Far East. This appointment had actually been agreed by the Prime Minister, Winston Churchill, more than a month before the War in the Far East broke out. It had been held up, however, by the Chiefs of Staff until now, when it was made largely on the insistence of Mr Duff Cooper, M.P., late Minister of Information in Britain[1], who had been specially sent out to the Far East by the War Cabinet in the early autumn of 1941 to report on the situation there.

Duff Cooper's original terms of reference had not included the military set-up. His task was to inquire into the civil administration of the various territories in the wide area under the British flag which stretched from the eastern border of India to New Zealand—and all of which he had duly, if briefly, covered and described.

Starting with Singapore, Duff Cooper had found an absurd duplication of activity in which two important officials, with their staff, were engaged on the same job of reporting to two different departments in London, the Ministry of Information and the Ministry of Economic Warfare. The most surprising thing, says Duff Cooper[2], was that there had been no trouble between them

> 'as the two men concerned were on good terms, lived in the same house, and showed one another everything they were doing. What they both objected to, however, was that neither of them had access to any naval or military information whatever, as this had been handed over by the Naval Authorities to an ex-naval officer, who had rejoined the service for the war, having spent the last

[1]In his autobiography, *Old Men Forget* (Rupert Hart-Davis, London).
[2]*Ibid.*

20 years as a magistrate in the Fiji Islands, and whose conception of his duties was to prevent anybody, especially the Americans, from obtaining any information whatever.'

Following his initial investigations in Singapore, Duff Cooper had made a swift tour of Malaya, Burma and India, as well as the Dutch East Indies and, later, of Australia and New Zealand. Convinced that war in this area was imminent, he had urged the appointment of a supreme Commissioner General for the Far East—and when the battle actually flared, of a Far Eastern War Council over which this officer would preside.

Duff Cooper had received no reply to his report (despatched on 1st November) when one night, more than five weeks later, he was awakened in Singapore by that first Jap air raid. Three days more, and a cable from Churchill informed him that he was himself appointed Resident Cabinet Minister at Singapore and authorised to form a War Council. Thereafter, for the first time, there was some kind of link between the Armed Services and the Civil Administration.

As Christmas fell on the fated North Malayan Front, the British rearguards were fighting their way back towards their next road-block bastion. This was at Kampar, a little market town which lies under the steep western slopes of a 4,000 ft. jungle mountain, about seven to eight square miles in area. Here, the re-formed 6/15th Brigade had dug hasty but well-sited defences to command both the northern approaches and the plain of rubber fields and open tin mine estates, which stretch away westward to the sea.

There were two possible military threats to this position, one fairly remote and the other very real. The **first** was that the Japanese would stab down along the narrow valley on the eastern side which separates this Kampar mass of rock from the main mountain watershed of Malaya, and by encircling it, would seal the garrison off from the South. The **second** danger was that, freed now from any strong resistance by British forces on the coast, the Japanese would bring in a seaborne invasion up the estuary of the Perak River, and by such means achieve the same object.

This latter possibility had, indeed, become more likely than ever in the days closely following Christmas. For by then, the last remaining British naval forces in North Malaya had disappeared.

These were the Perak Flotilla, consisting of the destroyer *Scout*, with some local craft, and a resolute seaborne raiding unit of about 50 Australians, known as 'Roseforce' from the name of the liaison officer attached to it[1]. Their task was to disrupt enemy communications west of the Perak River, and around Christmas they scored a triumph when, after a daring night voyage up the coast, they went ashore and ambushed a Jap convoy of three trucks, two vans and a staff car, in which were travelling some high-ranking Army officers.

A hundred per cent job. The car, which was leading, was hit by a grenade and crashed into the roadside trees. The ambush chief, Lieutenant R. E. Sanderson, poured a drumful of tommy gun ammunition into it, killing all the occupants. The first two lorries tumbled over the embankment, and their crews were also shot down as they tried to jump clear. The third lorry and the van halted, and the men in them scuffled away to what they hoped was the hiding of a near-by culvert. It turned out to be a trap, for the ambushers spotted them and in went a handful of grenades.

But alas! This was the end of Roseforce's 'bag.' A day or two later, the Japanese Air Force bombed and sank the flotilla's base depot ship H.M.S. *Kudat*, in the harbour at Port Swettenham. The knock-out blow followed on New Year's Day, 1942, when five fast 'Eureka' motorboats, which the Royal Navy had just acquired from the United States, were also bombed and sunk (or driven ashore) as they sped northward to reinforce the flotilla.

Whatever their fate, we should have kept Roseforce in being. For they were the sea equivalent of those com-

[1]Major A. J. C. Rose.

mandoes which, too late, we formed to fight on land, but which would subsequently provide the backbone of our 'Left Behind' Resistance Forces in Malaya.

On land, by the way, for the moment our fortunes seemed to be rather happier over the brief Christmas spell.

While the 6/15th Brigade slogged hourly to strengthen their defence works on the Kampar hillsides, the other two brigades of 11th Division (the 12th and the 28th) fought skilful delaying actions, and made the enemy pay dearly for his progress. By 26th December, the orderly evacuation of Ipoh Town had been completed, and much of the considerable military store pile which had been collected there at III Corps Headquarters since the opening of the campaign was either safely brought away or else destroyed. General Percival has made his own salute to the local civilian staffs who stayed to the end to do their duty:

> 'Among the last to leave their posts were the Chinese and Eurasian girl operators of the telephone exchange who were handling military traffic and who continued to do so in the face of bombing and the approach of the enemy until ordered to leave. All honour to them.'[1]

To hold the Kampar position, Maj.-General Paris, the new Divisional commander, now placed the lately-arrived 28th Brigade on his eastern flank, while he sent the 12th Brigade further down the road southward to Bidor, to guard against that ever-expected Japanese right hook from the sea.

It duly came, though only after the usual Japanese series of elaborate feints elsewhere. These had been already opened up on 30th December, when they sent their patrols probing around the entrance to the valley East of the Kampar mountain. Here, however, the Japs ran into the Gurkhas, who at last were on a terrain familiar to the Sons of Nepal, namely, steep, stony, scrubby hillside, and in savage slashing matches of Japanese sword and Gurkha *kukri*, the Sons of Nippon met their masters.

[1] In his book. See above.

But next day, New Year's Eve, our look-out posts on the
heights above Kampar Town observed far stronger enemy
forces moving around in the rubber estate to the South-west
of Kampar. Indeed, later came reports from our scouts, as
far as 30 miles away on the coast, that they were gathering
there, too. Here again, post-war research into Japanese
official files has revealed that their plan was, in fact, to launch
a frontal attack merely as a cover for a main encircling movement around our left flank.

It so turned out that this time it was those treacly pool-
deep swamps which proved too much even for the hard-
bitten, toughly trained Japs, and that sector of the
battle-front never caused the well-sited British garrison
any serious trouble.

Quite otherwise, however, was the outcome of that
originally planned 'deception attack' upon our centre and, as
it actually developed, upon our right flank at Kampar. This
opened at dawn on New Year's Day, and raged until long
into the night. In this relentless man-to-man struggle on
Thompson's Ridge, Green Ridge and Cemetery Ridge, the
recently combined British Battalion of the Leicesters and the
East Surreys earned a fame which still rings through the rival
armies who fought it out there.

General Percival has described the battle of the ridges in
vivid words, and with a conclusion worth nothing:

> 'The (enemy) attacks were made with all the well-known
> bravery and disregard of danger of the Japanese soldier.
> There was the dogged resistance, in spite of heavy losses,
> by the men of the British Battalion and their supporting
> artillery, and finally, when the enemy had captured a key
> position and the battalion reserves were exhausted, there
> was a charge in the old traditional style by the Sikh
> company of the 1/8th Punjab Regiment. Through a tre-
> mendous barrage of mortar and machine-gun fire they
> went, led by their company commander, Captain
> Graham, until he fell mortally wounded, and then by

their subedar. Their cheering rose to a roar as they charged, routing the enemy with heavy loss. The situation was completely restored, but only 30 of this gallant company remained. The battle of Kampar had proved that our trained troops, whether they were British or Indian, were superior man for man to the Japanese troops.'[1]

But while Fortress Kampar still held fast on the morning of 2nd January, the gateway at the rear was being smashed open.

On New Year's Day, one of our coast patrols had found a tug and four barges grounded on a sandbank at the mouth of the Perak River. The news was signalled to III Corps Headquarters, but by the time our bomber aircraft could arrive on the scene the tug and its convoy had been re-floated and sailed away. That same evening, a flotilla of seven small steamers, each towing several barges and landing craft, appeared in the mouth of the Bernam River (it is about six miles South of the Perak River) and landed one-and-a-half Japanese infantry battalions at the fishing village of Utan Melintang. They were engaged by our patrols, which they drove northward to Telok Anson, on the Perak River.

This irruption was alarming enough, for at Telok Anson the enemy was nearer to the main road and rail communications with the South than was the garrison of Kampar. But next morning, the news was worse.

The Japanese Invasion Force which had come by sea and been unshipped at Utan Melintang had been reinforced at Telok Anson by another battalion, which had come by raft down the Perak River!

Now though this Invasion Force was being held at the moment, it was plain that there was nothing to stop the Japanese bringing another battalion, brigade, or even a division into action by either, or both, of the same ways. General Paris had already been warned by the commander of

[1] In his book. See above.

the Kampar garrison that he could not hold on even there much longer, for the enemy was reinforcing on that front, too.

General Paris himself had no doubt as to what he must do. From Higher Command he sought, and obtained, permission to withdraw from Kampar while his force, however mauled and depleted, was still intact. There was much hard fighting yet to be done, if Central Malaya—and the vital link roads with our troops on the East Coast—was to be held.

As darkness fell on 3rd January, an army of almost sleep-walkers set off to trudge again through the night-hell of the jungle.

CHAPTER SEVEN

THE SLIM RIVER DISASTER

Were they treading towards safer ground—or into a trap?

It could be either.

For while the battle raged on the Kampar heights and along the banks of the Perak River, the Japanese were already probing 50 miles further South. There were prizes here well worth having—and they could be had for the taking, for the enemy now held complete command of both the sea and the air.

His first grab was at Kuala Selangor. Thence, roads run eastward through the coal mine area of Malaya known as Batu Arang and linking with the main North-South highway at Rawang; also down the coast to Port Swettenham.

General Heath had taken the precaution of arranging a really hot welcome party for the expected Japanese visitors at this river mouth, and when they duly arrived as darkness fell on 2nd January they were greeted by British gunfire, which sank one of their crowded troopships. The rest of the enemy craft hastily hauled off, and silence settled along that shadowy shore with its canopy of dark green trees.

But next night, the Japanese put in a landing party further up the coast and, by noon, they were driving our patrols back along the northern river bank towards the bridges at Batang Berjuntai, which is only a dozen miles from the main highway.

Hastily, General Heath reinforced his coastal flank guard,

Our Lockheed Hudsons go flying off to battle

British 25-pounders move up into action in a monsoon storm. (This is a flooded road, not a river!)

Australian infantry on patrol in the jungle and the rubber country

Spade work. A British Tommy trench-digging in the woodlands of Singapore Island as the Jap invaders draw near

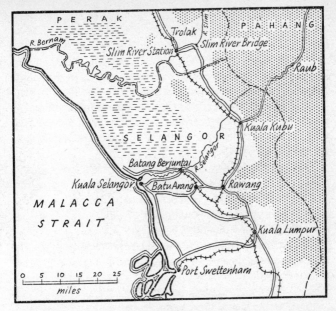

though the only troops he could spare for it were now almost physically dead-beat men of the Kampar Battle, the 6/15th Indian Brigade. They still managed to do the job of destroying the mining machinery and much of the piled-up stock of the Batu Arang coalfield, and thus withhold from the enemy a very valuable asset. They also blew the bridges at Batang Berjuntai, which would have been of even greater immediate strategic use to him.

For most of the 11th Division were still many miles northward, as, indeed, were the whole of the 9th Division, who had been engaged in the operations on the East Coast. Let us turn to them for a moment.

It is true that, by the New Year, our troops in the forward area were only of about brigade strength. They were spread round the port of Kuantan, though the bulk of them were withdrawn West of the Kuantan River where their task was to hold the airfield there as long as possible.

D

It was complicated by the fact that there are no roads southward from here, and the only way to travel by land in that direction is first to take the 200-mile road which runs westward via Jerantut and Raub to Kuala Kuba, in the State of Selangor, climbing over that backbone mountain range of Malaya to reach it and then follow the main North-South highway which passes through the centre of the town. Thus, if the Japs could strike in from the West Coast early enough, then they would sever the lifeline of the retreat of both the British divisions.

Bearing vitally upon these tactical problems was the desperate strategic need to deny the enemy the use of the Kuantan airfield until the first convoy of British reinforcements could arrive and disembark at Singapore. This was expected about the middle of January.

Two days still remained of the Old Year when the Japanese began attacking the outposts of 'Kuantan Force' (as the 22nd Indian Brigade's garrison there was officially known) with troops they had landed higher up the coast. There followed some fierce close fighting between them and the 2/18th Royal Garhwal Rifles, while the Japanese Air Force bombed the town, and still more the ferry over the river.

Fortunately, Brigadier Painter, the British commander, had split the ferry into two, and although one-half of it was sunk, the other was enough to carry our guns and transport across to the far bank that night. Next morning, the Japs made further determined efforts to capture the ferry but were held off until darkness descended once more, when the Garhwali rearguard did the last crossing of the river, and then the ferry was destroyed.

The respite gained was brief, for since this is the comparatively dry season in the mainland of Malaya the upper reaches of the stream are easily fordable—and they ran roughly parallel with the British line of retreat. During the next two days the enemy was pushing across strong patrols, and it seemed obvious that an attack would be mounted from that direction against the airfield, which is about eight miles west of Kuantan town.

By this time, 2nd January, the decision had been taken to withdraw the 11th Division from the Kampar position, so that unless the 9th Division also began to move towards that vital road junction at Kuala Kubu, then its fate was sealed. What else was now certain was that, even if the Kuantan Force fought on in the defence of the airfield, they could not hope to hold it until 10th January. General Heath therefore ordered withdrawal to the West.

The buildings and mechanical gear were pretty thoroughly demolished next day, then the main body of the Kuantan Force set off on their long march. But as night fell, the Japanese encircling troops closed in upon the airfield and the British rearguard of the 2/12th Frontier Force Regiment were very nearly trapped there.

Superbly led by Lt.-Col. A. E. Cumming, they managed to break through the ring, though with heavy casualties. Their commander was himself twice severely wounded, but borne along on a carrier, he moved from one danger spot to another, rallying his men by his example until, at length, he collapsed from loss of blood.

By this time, only 40 survivors made up the little band which accompanied their resolute leader. The enemy had now thrown ambushes and road-blocks across the British line of retreat, and these had to be cleared (or by-passed) if the battered rearguard were to rejoin their comrades. Not many of their number succeeded. For his own outstanding conduct and leadership on that night of blood and bravery, Lt.-Col. Cumming was awarded the Victoria Cross.

Something worthwhile had been salvaged.

First of all, though the Kuantan Force was slashed by a third of its strength, it still remained a fighting formation.

Next, though we did not know it at the time, the casualties inflicted on the enemy almost certainly outstripped our own.

Furthermore, by refusing the Japanese the use of Kuantan Airfield until the night of 3rd January, the garrison had enabled the first British reinforcement convoy to come in to Singapore that very afternoon, and disembark there without being bombed by near-based hostile aircraft.

Finally, the retreat of the 9th Division across the mountains to the West, was completed only just in time. For as the last units moved into the road junction of Kuala Kubu, they met a disorganised rabble pouring down from the North. These were the remnants of what had been the 11th Division.

Shattering defeat had fallen on them at the Battle of the Slim River.

We have seen how the British Commander had been compelled to dispatch the 6/15th Brigade to guard the West Coast river approaches to his left flank, while he fought a delaying action down the main road and railway to Kuala Kubu.

The 12th Brigade were disposed astride both, with wired defences, movable tank obstacles and weapon pits, in an area where they ran parallel to each other, a few hundred yards apart and bordered on either side by especially close-grown bush jungle.

The 28th Brigade were further down the road, in bivouac, at Slim River Village, where the country is much more open, being largely rubber estates, with their terraced rows of trees five or six yards apart.

And the troops of both brigades were flopping from fatigue, and such trench-digging as they were able to carry out, had to be done in the dark. For during daylight, the Japanese planes bombed and machine-gunned the open strips—and with never a single R.A.F. machine ever seen in the sky, such was our dreadful shortage.

Says Colonel C. C. Deakin, who commanded the 5/2nd Punjabis:

> 'The battalion was dead tired; most of all the commanders, whose responsibilities prevented them from snatching even a little fitful sleep. The battalion had with-

drawn 176 miles in three weeks and had had only three days' rest. It had suffered 250 casualties, of which a high proportion had been killed.'

The enemy opened action on 5th January with an infantry attack along the railway, which was repulsed with heavy loss and not renewed for two days. But in the meantime, the Japanese were operating their slick encirclement tactic, and refugees tramping south reported a massing of enemy armour further up the trunk road.

It was not until around midnight, 6/7th January, that the next assault came in.

This was delivered down both tracks, and was supported by heavy mortar and light machine-gun fire. The defending force of the 4/19th Hyderabads held firm until 3.30 a.m. when, in brilliant moonlight, a mixed column of tanks and lorried infantry followed by a marching column, surged like a tide along the highway. It swept across the not-very-well-built road-blocks of concrete cylinders, and overran our forward companies. Another enemy column of tanks and infantry poured down the railway.

Then luck, or maybe just a more effective enemy reconnoitre than our own, played a decisive part. For the Japs began to make use of certain disused loop roads where the main highway had been straightened out, and several times worked their way round to the rear of our positions. Then the tanks pounded down the main road, and not until they reached a deep trench across it which had been dug and mined by the 5/2nd Punjabis were they held up.

Here, with rifle fire, grenades and fire-bottles, the defenders assailed them. A madhouse medley developed. It has been described by Lt.-Col. C. C. Deakin:

'The leading tank struck the mines . . . and was wrecked. The din which followed defies description! The tanks behind were nose to tail—their engines roaring, their mortars and cannon firing all out.'

Several Japanese tanks were destroyed or knocked out, but then the enemy nosed round a second disused loop road and enveloped our position. A murderous hour followed.

The next disaster was the failure of the British sappers to destroy the main road bridge at Trolak village. By this time, all telephone lines in the forward area had been cut, and as we still desperately lacked wireless equipment in Malaya, the supporting troops of the 2nd Argylls were taken completely by surprise when the enemy tanks rolled in amongst them— and on towards the Slim River.

It was during this black-out of information that Maj.-Gen. Paris, the commander of the 11th Division, sent his senior Staff Officer, Colonel A. M. L. Harrison, forward from Headquarters to find out what was really going on. As he was motoring towards the front, he suddenly ran headlong into Japanese tanks, their machine-guns firing as they approached. Colonel Harrison's driver was hit, and slumped across the wheel of the car. A second or so before the leading tank crashed into it, Harrison himself leapt out and dived into the jungle border. The tank procession skirted past the wreckage, and raced on. Their break through was already several miles deep.

They owed this to their immense superiority in mechanised transport (and notably, pedal transport!). Consider this report by Lt.-Col. Spencer Chapman, then about to organise irregular warfare behind the Japanese lines, who was making his first visit to the jungle front. As he lay in a roadside thicket, he saw the enemy pouring by in hundreds:

'The majority of them were on bicycles in parties of 40 or 50, riding three or four abreast and talking and laughing just as if they were going to a football match. Indeed, some of them were actually wearing football jerseys; they seemed to have no standard uniform or equipment and were travelling as light as they possibly could. Some wore green, others grey, khaki or even dirty white. The majority had trousers hanging loose and enclosed in high

boots or puttees; some had tight breeches, and others
shorts and rubber boots or gym shoes. . . .
All this was in very marked contrast to our own first-line
soldiers, who were at this time equipped like Christmas
trees with heavy boots, web equipment, packs, haver-
sacks, water-bottles, blankets, ground-sheets and even
greatcoats and respirators, so that they could hardly
walk, much less fight.'[1]

Grim was the fate of our out-distanced survivors. The
casualty rate had been high in the battles, and as they fell back
there were added many more killed and wounded by enemy
snipers who had already snugged themselves up in the trees—
as well as those who, utterly exhausted, quit and surrendered.
Lt.-Col. Deakin himself, after a night-long trek through the
jungle, reached the Slim River with only three men.

They could not follow the road, which at this point turns
sharply eastward to Slim Village, because the Japs already lay
astride it. So, they went straight on down the railway line. By
now, this retreating remnant had been joined by stragglers,
and even 'lost' units, so that it numbered nearly a hundred
strong. They were still on the march the following night when
suddenly headlamps flared, and volleys of gunfire blasted
their ranks. The Japs had picked up their track. Only a
handful escaped again, the rest being killed or taken prisoner.
Among the captives was Deakin.

Another harsh experience was that of the commander of
the 36th Indian Field Ambulance. Early in the morning of
7th January, he rode off on his motor cycle to visit his
Advanced Dressing Station in the Trolak sector. Suddenly,
he ran into a column of 13 Japanese tanks lumbering along
the narrow, twisting road. He flung himself off his cycle,
dived into the rubber growth that bordered the track and
made his way to H.Q., 28th Indian Brigade. Picking up an
ambulance car, he called at the Advanced Dressing Station
and safely transported six men from there to H.Q., 2nd

---

[1] *The Jungle is Neutral*, by Lieut. Colonel F. Spencer-Chapman, D.S.O.

Gurkha Rifles. He had to swim across the slimy river to get to his Main Dressing Station, which he found blasted with gunfire though its personnel still laboured on. Back then to Brigade H.Q. just in time to see Japanese tanks shoot up its transport, and to learn that evacuation of casualties from the Trolak sector was now impossible. Once more this resolute officer returned to his Main Dressing Station to organise stretcher-bearer parties.

Ill-fortune dogged them, for they came under fire and had to break up. Later that night, they were forced to leave their wounded by the roadside and take to the jungle to try and get past the enemy road blocks. Only a handful succeeded. No Japanese mercy for the rest. They were chopped. *Bushido*.

Meantime, the Japs had pressed on along the road towards Slim Village and the key trunk road bridge beyond it which spans the Slim River. As the din of battle rolled over the jungle hills and gorges, the 28th Brigade had rushed to their action stations, though because of the breakdown of radio and telephone communications they still had no proper knowledge of what had happened in the sector held by the 12th Brigade further up the road.

It was too late to do their job. With an admirable audacity, the Japanese raiding force kept driving forward, though they were now far ahead of their supporting infantry. There was little, indeed, to stop them, for we had few anti-tank guns available and no effective grenades. By 8.30 a.m. on 7th January, the Japs had reached the Slim River road bridge. Since our sappers had received no warning signal it was still intact, and only a troop of light ack-ack artillery covered the approaches. Their shells simply bounced off the armour plate of the Japanese tanks, and the British gunners themselves were mown down by enemy fire. Though the invading column was shortly afterwards halted for several hours by one of our 155th Field Regiment howitzers, the bridge passed into Japanese hands and with it the key to Central Malaya.

It seemed that the British forces could do nothing right.

When our sappers did succeed in blowing up a bridge in time there was trouble. This happened with the railway bridge over the Slim River (one of the few which we managed to deny the enemy). After the massive girdered structure had crashed into the stream below a plank walk was hastily built across the gap. It proved inadequate to carry the traffic of weary and wounded men that crowded on to it, and further confusion was created when it came under enemy fire.

Because of the rush on the wobbling planks, many tried to wade or swim the dark, swirling stream, and were swept away and drowned. By nightfall, the 11th Division had suffered a fatal blow, for its 12th Brigade had practically ceased to exist and the 28th Brigade, too, was but a shadow. All their transport and most of their guns had been lost.

And the blame for this disaster? It would be easy to lay it on the failure to organise a more effective anti-tank defence, says General Percival, or to warn the troops in the rear of the break through up on the front, or to blow the bridge in time. But the real cause was the:

> 'Utter weariness of the troops, both officers and men. They had been fighting and moving by day and night for a month and few of them had had any proper rest or relief. To their physical fatigue was added a mental fatigue brought about by the enemy's complete supremacy in the air and on the sea and by a general sense of futility. In the exhausting and enervating climate of Malaya this was too great a test of human endurance and the troops had reached a stage when their reactions were subnormal.'[1]

Nor was the torment of this grim retreat yet ended.

[1]See his book.

CHAPTER EIGHT

RETREAT TO JOHORE

WHILE these military misfortunes were falling upon us in mid-Malaya, certain developments were taking place further South. Not all of these could be described as changes for the better.

To begin with, there was the arrival of the first British reinforcement. On 3rd January, there disembarked in Singapore Harbour the 45th Indian Infantry Brigade Group and a Pioneer battalion. This brigade had been part of the 17th Indian Division, led by a dynamic soldier and leader of men, Maj.-Gen. J. G. Smyth, V.C., M.C., who was himself destined to play a notable role in the retreat from Burma which was just about to begin. But not even 'Jackie' Smyth's skilled training had yet been able to do much to knock these troops into real fighting shape, for most of them had been enlisted only a few months earlier. Now, as their Commanding General in Malaya, General Percival found these reinforcements to be:

> 'Very young, unseasoned and under-trained, and straight off the ship after their first experience of the sea. Such training as the brigade had done had been for warfare in the open spaces of the Middle East, which had been its intended destination until war with Japan broke out. Only a short time before it left for Malaya its divisional commander had expressed his opinion that it was unfit for service overseas. It was typical of many formations and units which came to Malaya.'[1]

[1] See General Percival's book, quoted above.

106

It was to try and give these recently-recruited and totally unacclimatised troops a term of training in Malayan conditions of living in that sweaty drip-drip atmosphere of steam haze, within unhappy and unhealthy range of moths, mosquitoes, beetles, ants and snakes, within touch and tread of the jungle trees and the bamboo thicket and the mangrove swamp, within sound of its cacophony of crickets, owls, frogs, gibbon apes, wild boars, leopards, tigers and elephants— or in the more unearthly hours of silence which alternate with it—that General Percival sent them up to the State of Malacca, where barracks and camps already existed. Within a few days, they found themselves in hand-to-hand battle with the picked assault troops of the Imperial Japanese Army.

Now, even allowing for the crisis conditions which Japan's entry into the war had created, and the immediate shortage of available British troops (General Percival reminds us that '*the expansion of the Indian Army had not started until a year after the beginning of the war with Germany*'[1]), this sequence of events reflects no credit upon those who were directing War at the Top. It is surely almost incredible that the highest British military authorities should send as reinforcement to help hold Malaya against a formidable and ruthless enemy— and to strengthen the garrison of that 'impregnable Fortress Singapore'—units which were utterly unversed in jungle fighting or, indeed, in any other kind of fighting. And this was to continue.

Maj.-Gen. H. Gordon Bennett, commanding the Australian Imperial Force, has said that even the third batch of reinforcements, which arrived on 23rd January 1942 (the second came in on 13th January, of which more later), included Australian troops who had received practically no training at all. Some of these, in fact, had never before even fired a rifle. 'They were recruited on a Friday and were put on a boat for Malaya the following week', said Gordon Bennett.[2]

---

[1] See General Percival's book, quoted above. Author's italics.
[2] In an interview with the *Daily Express*—November 1957.

The Australian general has not confined his criticisms to the shortcomings of the other ranks in the British Army in Malaya, but has declared that he found a sad lack of 'aggressive spirit' in the unit commanders.

'This lack permeated some formations from top to bottom. Strong leadership at that time would have forced the issue or removed the officers concerned.'

Gordon Bennett and his titular superior, General Percival, were already not seeing too closely together.

Amongst other matters, Bennett wanted to have control of all troops in the State of Johore, should III Corps have to fall back there; alternatively, he suggested that all Australian troops be transferred to Western Johore, while III Corps took over the defence of Eastern Johore.

To neither of these propositions would Percival accede. On the one hand, he foresaw all kinds of difficulties of command and administration in what must have been an overnight fusion of the Australian Imperial Force with the British-Indian formation of III Corps. On the other hand, to shift the entire Australian contingent from the East Coast to the West Coast in the middle of active operations was to invite sure trouble.

On 5th January, Percival met the commanders of III Corps (Heath) and the A.I.F. (Bennett) in Staff conference at Segamat, Northern Johore. His purpose was to try and check the enemy's advance on Kuala Lumpur, capital of the Federated Malay States, and on Port Swettenham until at least the middle of January, thus keeping them off the airfields there until further British reinforcements had come into Singapore.

General Percival's plan was for III Corps, then, if need be, to fall back slowly by the West Coast roads into the State of Johore to the line of the twisting Muar River, which rises in the central mountain chain and for the last 60 miles of its course to the sea is spanned by not a single road or railway bridge. Behind this moat, which widens at Muar Town to

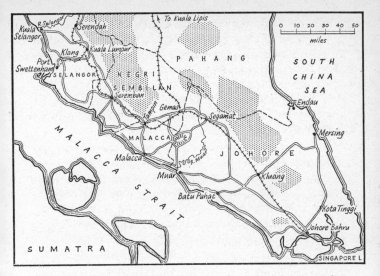

several hundred yards, Percival reckoned that the retreating British troops might make a real stand.

The danger was that if they were *too* slow in reaching it, the Japanese would get there first.

And, by now, the Japs had in active service both the necessary mechanised land transport and the seacraft to do this. The well-built road network in the States of Selangor, Negri Sembilan and Malacca offered the Japanese armoured columns ample opportunities to outflank our own foot-bound procession[1], while a landing on the coast as far down as Malacca might enable them to seize the town of Tampin, on the northern border of the State, which is the bottleneck through which all roads to Johore except one pass. Indeed, the possibility of the enemy landing on the West Coast of Singapore Island itself could no longer be overlooked (as for so long it had been!), and a look-out system was hastily improvised.

Having settled that the Muar River should cover his left

[1]There is ample evidence that the pre-war managers of the numerous Japanese estates in Southern Johore operated a plan on a grand scale to build motor roads *which all led to the coast opposite Singapore Island.* Author's note.

flank, from the Straits of Malacca inland towards the central mountains of Malaya, General Percival laid down the line of the rest of this new British front in Johore. It was to continue on to Segamat, which might fairly be described as its mid-sector, since the main North-South railway and the central trunk road run through it. Then it stretched onward over a forest hill land to Mersing, on the other coast, to complete the coverage of the right flank.

Arrangements were being worked out to relieve one of the Australian Brigades on this East Coast of Johore (where they had so far been doing only a completely uneventful garrison duty) and to shape them into a striking force for a counter-offensive the moment our reinforced strength permitted it, when right then the Slim River disaster crashed upon us.

To add to the turmoil (at any rate, at G.H.Q.!), on the very day of the battle, 7th January, General Sir Archibald Wavell arrived in Singapore on his way to Java to take up his post there as Supreme Commander, ABDA (American-British-Dutch-Australian) Command. He was off to the front early next morning to see for himself what was going on, and to judge the condition of the troops of III Corps who had survived the rout.

It was Wavell's opinion that, after a month's continuous fighting and retreating through the Malayan wilderness, their combat value was sinking dangerously low. To General Heath, who had accompanied him, he gave immediate verbal orders to withdraw the battlefront to the only-just-planned 'Percival Line' in North Johore. Returning to Singapore the same evening, Wavell saw Percival himself again and told him what he must do without further delay.

Next morning, Percival's own orders to his Army expressed in the necessary detail the Supreme Commander's general plan.

Firstly, this was designed to yield to the advancing enemy, without close engagement, the three West Coast States of Selangor, Negri Sembilan and Malacca—in order to conserve our limited strength to defend the tactically less vulnerable terrain of Northern Johore. The main body of III Corps was to be evacuated there by rail and road, leaving behind only enough mobile rearguards to cover demolition schemes.

Secondly, this 'Operation Evacuation,' as it were, of the tired veterans of the retreat was to be carried out through the screen of fresh troops who had never yet been in battle (though they were keen enough to go!) These were a battalion of the 27th Australian Infantry Brigade, who had been detached at Kota Tingghi in Johore—and being now relieved by an Indian battalion from Singapore—were to move across to the North-west frontier of Johore, where the next main assault was expected. The 22nd Australian Infantry Brigade remained on the East Coast until they, too, could be relieved by reinforcements from Singapore Island.

Meantime, the freshly-landed 45th Indian Infantry Brigade, which had just been posted to Malacca, moved up in partnership with the Australians on the West Coast. It was intended that when the 9th Indian Division, which had been the least severely mauled of III Corps, entered Johore from the North they should also be linked up with the Australians in this new formation, which was to be named 'Westforce' and be commanded by Gordon Bennett.

Finally, there was a curious division of the territory, though one explicable enough in the circumstances.

Thus, 'Westforce' was made responsible for operational control of that part of the front which stretched from the mouth of the Muar River up to the road and railway junction called Gemas, near its higher reaches in North Johore. Though this sector was only about one-third of the total breadth of Malaya, it was at this moment the only one where the enemy was engaged, and therefore 'Westforce' may be said to have provided the entire frontline garrison.

On the other hand, the responsibilities of General Heath's III Corps spanned the Malaya Peninsula from coast to coast, but their line was Batu Pahat—Kluang—Endau, which is between 40 and 50 miles to the rear. The reason for this has already been indicated; these troops of III Corps terribly needed some rest and recuperation. The disposition thus made conformed entirely with the Supreme Commander's instructions.

Meantime, The enemy had not been idle.

Since the New Year began, Japanese Army reinforcements from Siam and South China had been pouring into Malaya through the northern ports, and were now massing on the front for the next onslaught. In the air, the Japs reigned almost supreme, though small British bomber forces made audacious raids both on the enemy-held harbours and on his airfields.

Indeed, considering the now overwhelming strength of their numbers, the Japanese Air Force played a poor part in support of their troops in the field. True, because so often they swooped on our retreating or bivouacked columns unchallenged by our own fighters, they spread disorder and dispirit, lowering morale at a critical stage of the war in Malaya. But if they had ever been mobilised and deployed according to the standards of the Royal Air Force in Europe, in the Western Desert of Africa and, later, in the jungles of Burma, that retreat of ours through Malaya must have ended in a total scattering long before Singapore Island ever came in view.

It was General Wavell himself who said in a telegram to India Command at this time:

> 'Had the Japanese used their air superiority effectively there would have been complete disaster.'

In their bombing attacks upon the towns of Malaya, however, the Japs could claim real triumphs, Penang providing probably the most sensational in the Old Year. By the second week of the New Year, Singapore was starting to move in the same direction, with almost regular daylight attacks upon the City, the Harbour or the neighbouring airfields on the Island.

The enemy was immensely helped, of course, not only by our own loss of look-out posts on the mainland as the British troops fell back but by a hopelessly inadequate radar cover,

which failed to give anything like the 30-minutes warning
needed to enable our out-of-date Buffalo fighters to climb to
the 20,000 feet at which the Japanese bombers flew in.

By contrast, General Gordon Bennett tells in his book[1]
of a Japanese 'guider' radio set which was known to be hidden
somewhere near the Johore Causeway and giving regular
service to the incoming raiders. (It could never be located
because we had no instrument in Malaya which could pin-
point it, and though urgent requests were made no detector
apparatus ever arrived from England.)

Add to these deficiencies, the fewness in Singapore Island
of ack-ack batteries of 3.7 inch guns capable of ranging the
Japanese bombers, and—as they closed to within fighter aircraft reach of this latter target—the superiority of their Zero
planes over our Buffaloes, and the marvel is that Singapore
was not lost before the retreating British Army in Malaya
ever arrived back there.

So much for Japanese activities by land and in the air.
The enemy did not neglect the third element—the sea. Plans
were made to land an invading force, which mustered about
the strength of a division, on the North-eastern coast of
Johore towards the end of January. This was to coincide with
the seizure of the Anamba Islands, about 150 miles off-shore
in the South China Sea, which the Japanese Navy needed as
an advanced base for the final assault on Singapore Island.

On the West Coast, too, the Japs were busy. North of the
Selangor River, on 4th January, they had put ashore at least a
battalion of infantry equipped with bicycles. Four days later,
they attempted another landing at the river mouth, but this
time their open boats were sunk by fire from a battery of the
22nd Mountain Regiment of the Indian Artillery.

That midnight, however, the enemy crossed Selangor River
upstream, encircled our positions on the South bank, and by
dawn had overrun them and stormed into the town of Kuala
Selangor, over-running the H.Q. of the 1/14th Punjab Regi-

---

[1] *'Why Singapore Fell,'* by Lieut. General H. Gordon Bennett (Angus &
Robertson Ltd.).

ment. Once more, a valuable strategic area had to be abandoned.

British withdrawal plans were not working out too well. The military evacuation of Kuala Lumpur had been going on for several days but huge stocks of petrol, oil, coal and rubber as well as factory and mine machinery could not be shifted. They had to be burned or blown up if the enemy was not to take them over. So a mighty bonfire advertised the departure of the British Raj from the capital of the Federated Malay States, and signalled the arrival of the new masters from Nippon.

Indeed, the line of our retreat was all too often a pathway of flame, for Japanese agents (or sympathisers) were ever active in setting fire to the *kampong* (village) huts of wood and palm thatch, or the bamboo *bashas* on their stilts. These could easily be replaced later on, but their destruction now would be a useful addition to current chaos. This local sabotage act, therefore, was pretty thoroughly done.

Effective, too, was the way in which the Japanese so often managed to outpace the retreating British and to throw themselves across our track—or rather, tracks, for we pursued two main ones. The first of these was the principal North-South trunk highway; the second was the winding coastal road.

Thus, on 10th January, as at dawn the 28th Brigade fell back under heavy artillery and air attack from Serandah village, 15 miles North of Kuala Lumpur, they found the road already in enemy hands. Not until nightfall were the remnants of the brigade able to fight their way, through a drenching wall of rain, to the outskirts of the town. Here, the 6/15th Brigade, which had also suffered severe losses in a battle among the coastal chaungs, provided a resolute rearguard to cover the withdrawal from Kuala Lumpur itself. This was carried out in the next few hours, and at 4.30 a.m. the last bridge in the town was blown up with a shattering roar that echoed across the mountain range.

A desperate problem at this time was that of evacuating the wounded. Road transport was lacking and an ambulance train service had to be improvised out of ordinary rolling stock. Carriages were gutted and fitted out with sling stretchers. The trains were short of kitchen and even lavatory facilities. Driven for the most part by those ever-handy naval survivors from H.M.S. *Prince of Wales* and H.M.S. *Repulse*, they often took 18 hours to do a journey of 200 miles on the overtaxed railway—or about 11 miles per hour. Sometimes trolley cars, loaded with casualties were pushed by hand down the line.

A tale of personal adventure that lights up this dark record of general misadventure is that of Captain P. North, of the 3rd. Dogra Regiment.[1]

Along with the 2/9th Gurkha Rifles, two companies of the Dogras manned the defences of Serandah. Lacking any proper entrenching tools, they had been obliged to dig themselves in—during a night of downpour—with some hoes which they found in the village and their own bayonets. Attacked in force at dawn, and with close air-bombing, the garrison was slowly driven back from Serandah. All communications with the rear being snapped, Captain North, who was at Brigade H.Q., offered to go forward and try to get in touch with his battalion. Two Gurkha soldiers volunteered to accompany him, and together they set off in a carrier.

Soon, they were in the enemy's midst. The carrier was overturned, killing one of the Gurkhas. North and the other one crawled from under the wreck, saw a Japanese gun crew firing a few yards away—and crawled back. They stayed there all day in a ditch. Night fell. They slipped away, and in a village hut got some native clothes. Then off again, into the green Shadowland, headed southward.

Five days later, they were picked up by a Japanese patrol, and shot.

But, at sun-peep next morning, North opened his eyes again. He had only been wounded. So had his Gurkha comrade. They made their way to a rubber estate near Kuala

<hr />

[1] It has been told by Sir Compton Mackenzie, in his book *Eastern Epic*. Vol I. Chatto & Windus, London.

Lumpur, where friendly coolies hid and fed them for a week. Then, North being now fit to go, he said good-bye to these fine friends and departed alone. He had covered a hundred miles before the Japs took him prisoner again as he crossed a golf-course. This time, they kept Captain North in their hands until the end of the war.

We return to the battle in the West. In the coastal area, the Japs planned to seize the towns of Port Swettenham and Klang by a simultaneous landward advance from Kuala Selangor and a seaborne assault at the mouth of the river. This time, the downpour certainly favoured us, for the main body of the Japanese land force was still on the march up country when the sea invaders arrived at the port. A much mixed-up engagement developed, after which the enemy tried to outflank the British garrison at the Klang bridgehead. This only partly succeeded, for the British moved out before the trap could be sealed. But two of our columns were caught in ambush further along the road that night, and paid heavy penalties. The British sappers' attempt to blow the great bridge over the river was badly handled, and all too soon the Japs had repaired it.

The retreat went on.

Oddly, for the next three days, it was not harassed by the enemy—except, to some extent, by his aircraft. The much-slashed units of III Corps passed in comparatively good order behind the shield of 'Westforce,' and went into reserve for a breathing space.

Would it be long enough for the entire British Forces in Malaya to rally, and strike back a smashing blow at an invader who was already several hundred miles away from his nearest bases?

It might well have been so—if averagely intelligent action had been taken at topmost Service levels to tackle the problem. It was not. The tale of the British reinforcement of 'Fortress Singapore' at this hour would be farcical, if it were not so tragic.

For though on 13th January, there had arrived in Singapore the second reinforcement convoy of infantry, artillery and fighter aircraft, the greater part of it had better never have been unloaded.

The infantry were the 53rd Brigade Group of the 18th British Division, a second-line Territorial formation which had sailed from England the previous October, bound for the Middle East. When the war with Japan broke out, they were off the East coast of Africa and from there were diverted to Malaya. So now they had been at sea for nearly three months, and, as General Percival remarks, 'although fit, were naturally very soft.' Very few of them had ever been abroad before, and almost none of them had been in the Tropics. Absolutely none whatever had been trained in jungle fighting. They arrived without their transport, which was following in a slower convoy.

The artillery consisted of the 6th Heavy and 35th Light British Anti-Aircraft Regiments and the 85th British Anti-Tank Regiment. They arrived without their guns.

The aircraft were 51 Hurricanes in crates. They were not of the most modern type. With them came 24 pilots, not one of whom had ever had any experience of flying in Malayan conditions.

General Percival reckoned that the 18th Division could not be deployed as such to fight on the mainland at the earliest before the end of the first week in February, i.e. three and a half weeks ahead. *Could 'Westforce' hold the enemy on the Johore border for as long as that?*

The very next day, 14th January, the struggle for Johore opened.

CHAPTER NINE

THE BATTLE OF MUAR

GENERAL Gordon Bennett's 'Westforce' had now taken up position, covering the front from the mountains to the shore of the Malacca Straits. *Positions*, perhaps is a truer word, for there were two main areas, and both of these were sub-divided into sectors, which were themselves sometimes widely separated and linked with each other chiefly by rather tenuous signal communications.

No. I Area was around the central trunk road and the railway beyond Segamat.

Its three sectors were: (a) astride both road and railway near Gemas. Here, the 8th Indian Brigade made up the holding force. Next, (b) was further forward along the same road, where the 27th Australian Brigade lay. They were charged with a counter-offensive role, and had already prepared an advanced ambush for the enemy several miles ahead. The remaining sector, (c) was to the leftward, where the 22nd Indian Brigade guarded the approaches to Segamat from Malacca, which skirt either side of Mount Ophir.

No. II Area was that which covered the West Coast and the roads which run along it to Johore Straits. This had two sectors, actually more in line with one another than those of No. I Area, but even less effectively in touch.

The defence of this area was entrusted to the 45th Indian Brigade, reinforced by a single battery of field artillery. It included the seaport of Muar, and stretched some 30 miles up into the jungle towards Segamat, along the winding course of the Muar River, with its deep-wooded, creeper-covered banks. Under orders from General Gordon Bennett, two of the battalions were disposed along the river line, which they thus divided between them, while the third went into active reserve near the coast.

We have already noted that this 45th Indian Brigade was newly-arrived in Malaya (indeed, it was only recently raised, and several of its company commanders had not even passed a language test). Apart from the fact that practically all of these troops, too, were totally unversed in bush warfare, again most of them were unblooded in any kind of fighting whatever.

To deploy them along a front of such length was surely a serious tactical error?

(Indeed, they were soon still further dispersed, in depth, when the Brigade Commander was ordered to set up outpost positions on the northern bank of the river and to garrison them with a couple of companies from each of the forward battalions). But Gordon Bennett seems to have been obsessed with the idea that the enemy was going to use any available jungle track, footpath, or even brook, to by-pass the defence and break their line of communication. The trouble was that 'Westforce' could not provide the strength to place a fixed guard on every avenue. Had they possessed in this region only a few hundred men skilled in jungle patrol, the story might have been very different.

With the ambush laid by the 27th Australian Brigade on the trunk road beyond Gemas we scored more success. Here, on our side of a wooden bridge spanning a stream, a company of the 2/30th Australian Battalion had entrenched and concealed themselves. The bridge itself had been mined, and a battery of field artillery sited on some higher ground behind our infantry whence it could command the enemy approach to the bridge. The Australian battalion, under Lt.-Col. Galleghan, had spent some energetic weeks earlier while on garrison duty in Eastern Johore practising these tactics. (This particular ambush was laid under General Percival's own instructions; he strongly felt that ambush was the way to fight the Japanese).

It was about 4 o'clock in the afternoon of 14th January, when the advance guard of the enemy approached—mounted on bicycles. They flowed across the bridge, into the ambush area, and beyond it. Then came the main Japanese column, several hundred strong, also cycling, and followed by tanks and engineer trucks. At this point, the bridge went up with a blast, and timber, bicycles and bodies hurtled through the air, while from the ambush lane and the anti-tank traps further on there poured a devastating fire, mowing the procession down like grass by the roadside.

Heavier still would have been the Japanese losses but for a slice of good luck to them—or a piece of poor camouflage by us. For some of the enemy who had passed through the ambush area, spotted in the patchy undergrowth of the jungle's edge the field telephone cable which ran back to our gun positions, and promptly cut it. So our artillery received no signal of any kind, and never came into play at all.

It was not long, by the way, before the enemy guns from beyond the stream were ranging on the road. (The fact that it was cluttered with their own dying and wounded fellow-countrymen did not enter into the consideration of the Japanese Command; any soldier of Nippon who could no longer march or fight expected no more regard from the Imperial Army than was given by them to an enemy casualty or prisoner-of-war). The Australian ambush party, having done a substantial slaughter, duly fell back in several groups that same evening and by next day had rejoined their battalion in the position near Gemas.

On this morning of 15th January, the Japanese aircraft were dive-bombing them heavily, and also the town of Gemas itself. Indeed, already by 10 a.m. enemy infantry were attacking our lines, and as the day wore on they were supported by an increasing number of tanks. So the Japanese sappers had wasted no time, either, in repairing the wrecked bridge. It was one more example of their very efficiently organised engineer service.

The Australians continued to repel all assaults, throwing one of them, indeed, into chaos by a resolute counter-attack. But enemy reinforcements were now steadily rolling up. As night fell, Lt.-Col. Galleghan withdrew his battalion along the Gemas-Segamat road. They had shown what trained troops could do against the fabled Japs, inflicting upon them extremely disproportionate losses. The Australian withdrawal was in no way harassed by the enemy, and for the next day or so quiet settled over the Segamat area.

Not so over the Muar area, on the other flank of the 'West-force' front. Here, during the last few days and nights, had developed an ever-increasing activity—and a further series of setbacks to the British arms.

It opened on 11th January, when the Japs began bombing the seaport of Muar, at the mouth of the river of that name.

This set off the same kind of general exodus of local labour as had afflicted Penang and other places which had come under the enemy's air flail. Early to go were the Asian employees of the waterworks and of the power station. Almost as soon—and their loss was the more serious—went the crews and the pier hands of the Muar vehicle ferry.

For this ferry, which is several hundred yards wide, is the only method of shifting heavy goods or transport across the Muar River, from its estuary to a point perhaps as far as a hundred miles upstream. It will be realised that Muar Ferry thus provided a key service. This had now to be operated by a company of British sappers, whose wholetime work was already required on jobs preparing road bridges for demolition, building runway blocks on abandoned airfields and other potential landing grounds, making river booms, and laying booby-traps.

The bombing of Muar went on daily until the morning of 15th January, when Japanese troops of the crack 5th Guards Regiment, advancing from Malacca suddenly appeared in the low-lying coastland on the northern bank of the river, where

they took by surprise and totally overran the forward companies which had been posted there by the 45th Indian
Brigade (they belonged to the 7/6th Rajputana Rifles, perhaps
the rawest of our troops). No alarm signal of any kind ever
reached Headquarters. At 11 a.m. the Japs arrived on the
waterfront opposite Muar Harbour.

It was not the only approach which they had made. Moving
on Muar Town from a little higher up the river, was a second
column which would shortly make the crossing. And, already
at sea, were a number of boats sailing from Malacca which
would put ashore that afternoon small parties of infantry
South of Muar and, later, even further down the coast
beyond the next port of Batu Pahat, where they occupied the
lighthouse.

That night, 15/16th January, a handful of Japanese raiders
paddled silently across the Muar above the town in sampans
and on bamboo rafts which they had picked up from the
near-by ricefields. On the southern bank, they climbed aboard
a number of barges which were moored there, slipped the
cables and towed them overstream where a bridgehead force
was waiting to embark in them.

Neither the sneaking of these barges nor their return an
hour or two later, laden with enemy troops, seems to have
been spotted by the defenders. The only resistance which the
invaders met was a subsequent brush with an Indian patrol,
which retired after a brief exchange of shots—and also failed
to report to Headquarters the arrival of the enemy on the
South bank.

It was not long, indeed, before they made their presence
felt, and painfully. As day broke, this Japanese outflanking
force had taken by surprise a company of the 7/6th Rajputana Rifles (while they lay in bivouac) and had routed
them. By noon, the Japs were attacking from upstream both
Muar Town and the garrison's line of communications with
its only reserve battalion, which was located near Bakri, on
the main road south from Muar. The commander of that
battalion, by the way, was ambushed and killed as he

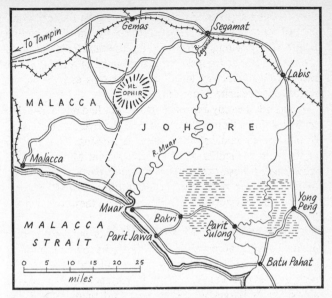

travelled along the road this very morning. Soon afterwards, the Japs had streamed across it.

Further forward, things were going no better.

True, at Muar itself, an enemy attempt to land and seize the harbour had been blown out of the water by the Australian gunners of our single battery of field artillery in this area, firing over open sights at the packed barges and junks as they tried to make their way across the river mouth.

But these same would-be invaders had already mopped up the two forward companies of the Indian battalion covering the lower reaches of the river (which Gordon Bennett had insisted should be disposed upon its northern bank), and now in the late afternoon the Japs, who had already made the crossing higher up, stormed into Muar Town and captured the garrison headquarters. The battalion commander, the second-in-command, and almost all the company officers were killed. By nightfall, Muar Town and Harbour had passed into the hands of the enemy. The remnants of the garrison made off down the coast several miles as far as Parit Jawa, where they turned inland to the crossroads at Bakri.

Here, the main body of 45th Indian Brigade were now concentrated, for the second of the battalions along the Muar River line (they were the 4/9th Jats) had been able to withdraw its forward battalions from the far bank without losses. The Brigade strength was still far below that required for its duties, and these were now vital.

For 30 miles rearward of Bakri lies the jungle village of Yong Peng, through which ran the only road linking 45th Brigade with the rest of 'Westforce,' who were still massed between Gemas and Segamat. The threat to this was obvious, and Gordon Bennett hastened to withdraw the reserve battalion from the 27th Australian Brigade in that area, and motor it down by lorry to reinforce the Muar front. This reinforcement arrived within 24 hours.

General Percival also took some swift decisions. Reckoning that Gordon Bennett had more than enough to do to control the widely separated sectors of his 'Westforce' front, Percival ruled that III Indian Corps should take over the protection of his communications against both shore and jungle forays by the enemy. To provide the needed forces, Percival ordered up from Singapore the 53rd British Infantry Brigade Group, which had only been disembarked at the port three days earlier, after nearly three months at sea in crowded troopships where they got no exercise whatsoever.

General Percival has been castigated for these dispositions; by Gordon Bennett, who wanted the freshly-arrived British Brigade to relieve his 22nd Australian Brigade on the East Coast so that they could join up with the rest of the Australians in 'Westforce,' and by other critics who have stressed the complete unfamiliarity of the new British troops with Malayan terrain conditions and condemned their hurried dispatch to the front.

To the first criticism, Percival has made reply that there simply was not time to switch the 22nd Australian Brigade over to the West Coast (though he did actually move another Australian battalion there the very next day).

To the second criticism, actual events have provided the answer. It had, indeed, been intended that the newcomers should begin by guarding the lines of communication in the 'Westforce' area, which was what they would have been doing in Eastern Johore if they had relieved the Australians there. But even if this had happened, they would not have been confined to watch duties for very long—or have had much time to train there in jungle tactics.

For the Japanese invaders had not overlooked this way to Singapore, either, although there was not a single road down the East Coast until one began at Endau. This in itself was no serious handicap to the Japs, with their now unchallenged command of the sea—provided, of course, they could get themselves a forward base to unload their artillery, transport and stores. Endau would serve this purpose, therefore towards that little port enemy mobile columns made their way.

From the British point of view, Endau was not easily defensible at this stage. So, as the Japs massed North of the town and steadily bombed it, the commander of the 22nd Australian Brigade decided to withdraw to a position which had been prepared beyond the river at Mersing, about 25 miles further down the East Coast, destroying all bridges and culverts as they went. No major encounter developed as yet, but the increasing patrol and skirmish activity, especially at night, indicated that something was afoot. As indeed it was! If these untrained (for bush war) and unacclimatised fresh units from Britain had been posted to eastern Johore, they would have been thrown into battle there within a week.

Instead, posted to the West Coast, what was their fate?

Arrived in the rear of 'Westforce,' the 53rd British Brigade was distributed between the coastland round Batu Pahat, where, as we have noted, a Japanese raiding party had for a time occupied the lighthouse (they had since concealed themselves in a near-by rubber estate) and a narrow defile on the Bakri-Yong Peng main road.

Each was a key position. For the first guarded the open sea-flank of this leftward, No. II Area of the 'Westforce' front; and the second guarded its main line of communication, both rearward and with the rightward, No. I Area of 'Westforce' inland around Segamat. A special, new importance attached to the former area because a British counterattack had just been planned there.

This was because Percival was convinced that either this part of the front must be stabilised, or else the entire Segamat Force be withdrawn. Otherwise, their actual survival might be imperilled.

Now Percival feared—and in this, Gordon Bennett agreed with him—that to set off in retreat again at this moment would be to deal another deadly blow at the morale of the whole army. The Australians had just gone into action, with marked success. The British and Indian troops, after a very rough handling up-country, were beginning to settle down and every day that we held fast improved their condition. (But, remember, there was always this danger in hanging on to our present front—that the enemy, with his vastly superior means of transport, might cut our long line of communication with Singapore Island). It was resolved to take this chance. General Percival took a further one when he sent the 2/19th Australian Battalion across from Eastern Johore to join 'Westforce.'

So orders went forth to the 45th Indian Brigade to recapture Muar. Following their earlier mishaps in the fighting along the river banks, these troops had rallied around Bakri and within a few hours had organised a rough perimeter defence of it. Their Commander, Brigadier H. C. Duncan, now planned a trident advance from it upon Muar; up the main road between the towns, from the jungle island, and along the coast road.

The attack went wrong before it could be launched. For the Japs had forestalled our preparatory movement along the coast, laying another of their ambushes there for the Garhwali Rifles. Before midnight, 17/18th January, the British counter-offensive had been cancelled.

By contrast, the enemy went right ahead with his. That same evening, the Japanese Commander, General Nishimura, ordered his own three-spear attack on Bakri, and by dawn the Japanese light tanks were in action on the main road. They had the worst of a tussle with the Australian artillery, losing eight machines, but their infantry managed to seep round our flanks and even to set up a road block for a time just behind our front. Close fighting went on all day.

Meantime, British Intelligence reported that the enemy had now got two full divisions deployed in the front line. One, in the Muar coastal area, belonged to the Imperial Guards. The other, in the up-country Segamat area (oddly enough), was the 5th Division, which had been specially trained in landing operations. A sheaf of alarm signals told of enemy patrols behind our lines, chiefly in the region of Batu Pahat. An invasion here, of course, could not only cut off 45th Brigade but might threaten the whole of 'Westforce,' whose main line of communication (and of retreat) lay within 20 miles of it.

There was a grim telephone talk that night between Percival and Gordon Bennett. The Commander-in-Chief agreed with the leader of 'Westforce' that without delay it should be withdrawn behind the Segamat River, and that further retreat was likely to be necessary. Because these operations would demand the day-and-night surveillance by Bennett as the responsible executive officer, Percival insisted that the Muar sector of the front be placed temporarily under III Indian Corps. It will be realised that by now there was a considerable job of co-ordination to be done here.

Next morning, it had multiplied. The Japanese force on the coast beyond Bakri, which had unhinged that British plan to re-take Muar, were now attacking our Bakri perimeter position and had already cut the road behind it. Most of our transport they captured, or burned. Then a direct hit by a

Japanese bomber pretty well wiped out Brigade headquarters. Repeated infantry assaults went on all the afternoon.

It became plain that unless the British forces were withdrawn from this now practically-encircled area, they would either be captured there or annihilated. Orders went forward to them by radio to retire along the Bakri-Yong Peng main road.

Too late! The enemy already lay across the road, and at its most difficult and dangerous point. This was about five miles West of Yong Peng, where it runs on a long causeway across a swamp, then enters a defile between two wooded ridges. Here, it is joined by a road which comes up from the South and Batu Pahat. This place was obviously of prime tactical value.

It had been garrisoned for the past day or two by the 6th Norfolk Battalion of the recently arrived 53rd British Brigade. Early in the afternoon of 19th January, a Jap raiding force took them by surprise and drove them off the lower slopes of the ridges on either side of the road. A company of the Norfolks, after a stubborn resistance, retired up through the thick jungle to the summit of the northern ridge. Being without wireless, they were unable to inform battalion headquarters of their position, which turned out tragically.

For in the grey light of dawn next morning, the 3/16th Punjabis, ordered to 'recapture' this ridge, had just reached the crest when they came under withering fire, and then were charged by the garrison—who were the Norfolks (and who had mistaken *them* for the enemy). After losses on both sides, this was somehow sorted out. But before a proper defence could be organised, the Japanese had also arrived from down below and they now drove both the British and Indian troops off the hill.

Meantime, crashing blows had fallen upon the men of the 45th Indian Brigade in the Bakri region.

First, there was that battalion (the 4/9th Jats) which had been originally assigned to guard the higher reaches of the Muar River, and had so far managed to withdraw in good

A.I.F. (Australian Imperial Forces) in the near-jungle of Eastern Malaya setting up barbed-wire entanglements

Australian ambulance men bearing away a wounded comrade

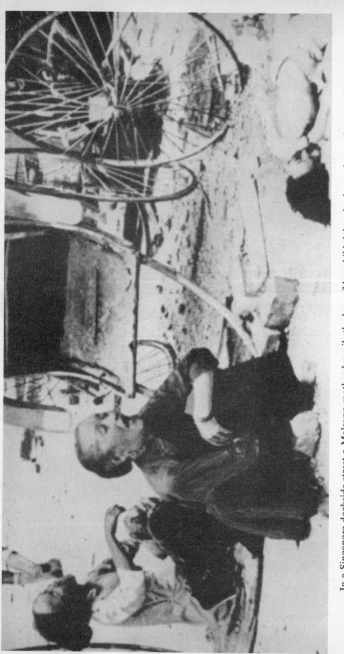

In a Singapore dockside street a Malayan mother bewails the loss of her child, lying dead near by on the spot where a Japanese bomb fragment struck her

order to the North of the Bakri perimeter. But on the afternoon of the 19th, as they closed in upon the main position,
they were ambushed. The commander, his adjutant and
many company officers were among the first casualties of the
opening volley of machine-gun and rifle fire. Wrote General
Percival of the scene of tumult and disorder which ensued:

> 'The young Indian recruits were helpless. They did not
> even know how to take cover, and there were not enough
> officers to control them. I say this in no spirit of dis-
> paragement. It was the penalty of years of unprepared-
> ness for war coming out in all its stark nakedness.'[1]

There was a heavy hammering, too, for the 2/29th Australian Battalion, who had been front line neighbours of the Jats.
After repulsing very heavy pressure on their own position by
a sharp counter-attack, the Australians also set off later that
evening for Bakri. Ambush awaited them, too, and in the
cloak of a jungle night. Only about 200 men rushed or groped
a passage past the enemy and reached Bakri. The rest were
killed, or captured, or drowned, as they tried to wade their
way across the marshes to distant Yong Peng.

The third and final disaster on the Muar Front encom-
passed the main fighting force in the line there, which was
still the 45th Indian Brigade.

It had been hastily re-organised overnight by Lt.-Col. C. G.
Anderson, of the Australian Imperial Force, acting for
Brigadier Duncan, and now consisted of an Australian
battalion of five companies and an Indian battalion made up
of the survivors of the three original Indian battalions.

Early in the morning of 20th January, they began their
march out from Bakri towards Yong Peng. Within a mile or
so, they were held up by enemy road barriers. Several efforts
to break through failed, until a bayonet charge led by
Lt.-Col. Anderson was successful. But this fighting had checked
the march for a couple of hours, and now the enemy were
squeezing hard upon our rear and had brought up tank

[1] See his book.

reinforcement. It was to repel one of these attacks that Brigadier Duncan insisted on returning to active service. He was killed, leading a bayonet counter-charge, a truly gallant officer.

More road blocks lay ahead and had to be cleared, in what General Percival had described as 'some of the fiercest and most terrific fighting of the whole campaign.'[1] By sunset, after a struggle which had raged on throughout all the hours of daylight, the column had covered a distance of only about three miles.

There was to be no rest that night. Lt.-Col. Anderson, who had taken over command of the brigade again, ordered the march to go on. They had now reached the edge of some rather more open country and passage was easier, though the column was laden with many wounded.

It was after midnight that scouts reported fresh trouble ahead. Now the bridge over the next river, at the village of Parit Sulong, was in the hands of the enemy! This had happened because the guard which had been placed there by the 6th Norfolks, being cut off from all contact with them since the Jap raiding force drove the battalion from the defile a few miles further on, had left their post and set off along the river bank to Batu Pahat.

Dawn had broken before the 45th Brigade could mount an attack upon the enemy position covering the Parit Sulong bridge, and when this failed a new (and much harder) clinch developed upon our rear. For now the Japs brought up heavy tanks, and backed with artillery and low-flying aircraft they forced our column into an area measuring only about a quarter-of-a-mile of roadway. Fighting raged all day, and our casualties were very severe.

At dusk, with the dead and dying piling up all round, Anderson sent two ambulances filled with the most dangerously wounded men to the bridge under a flag of truce, asking that they be allowed to pass through to the British lines beyond. The Japanese reply was to demand the surrender of the column, with the promise that the wounded would then be

[1] In his book. See above.

cared for. Meantime, added this chivalrous voice of *Bushido*, the ambulances were to remain on the approach to the bridge, to act as a road block—and they would be fired on if they attempted to move!

Our men outwitted the Japs (though, later, it seems they paid a bitter price for it). For after dark, an officer and a driver, both of whom were themselves wounded, slipped the brakes of the ambulances, and let them run silently backwards down the slope from the bridge. Then, amid the roar of the guns, they started up their engines and drove them back to the column.

Next morning, as the sun rose, some relief came down from the skies. For a couple of R.A.F. planes, flying from Singapore in answer to the desperate appeals, skirted low over the rubber-fields and dropped both medical supplies and food rations on the trapped 45th Brigade.

But from the skies, too, came a fresh tornado of bombs and machine-gun fire, as the Japanese aircraft joined with their tanks and field artillery in another bombardment of the shrinking British foothold.

Now, the end was near. There was one last attack on the bridgehead by the Australians. It failed, and at 9 a.m. Anderson gave orders for all guns, vehicles and equipment to be destroyed, arranged for the many wounded who could not walk to be left behind in the care of voluntary attendants, and told the remnants of the brigade to take to the jungle and try and find some path back to Yong Peng. Eventually, about 500 Australians and 400 Indians got through, out of an original brigade strength of more than 4,000.

And the wounded who had to be abandoned to the mercy of the enemy? The Japanese, after treating them with bestial savagery, massacred in cold blood all except a handful who feigned death and, later, crawled away to escape.

This was the fate of the men of an Australian ambulance-column, who were captured after a three-day-and-night roundabout trek along jungle by-ways to try and make their way back to the main British forces. With kicks, clouts and curses, blows from rifle butts and bayonet jabs, their captors crammed them all into a couple of small rooms in a coolie hutment at Parit Sulong village on the Muar highway. The wounded lay piled upon one another's bodies on the earthen floor. They were denied drinking water by the Japs, who also mocked them by bringing along bucketfuls of it as far as the doorway—and then pouring it out upon the ground.

Later, a special convoy of Japanese Army staff officers arrived, escorted by a troop of medium tanks. A senior officer dismounted, peered through the open door, gave some brief orders, and then drove off.

The prisoners-of-war were promptly trussed up into small groups with rope or wire, pushed into the roadside scrub at the point of the bayonet, and machine-gunned there. Afterwards, a number of the Japanese guards walked back to the roadway, and picked up some tins of petrol. This was flung over the bodies of the shot prisoners, some of whom still lived, and then set alight.

The hideous story is told by Lieutenant Ben Hackney, of the 2/29th Battalion, Australian Imperial Force, who was there and only escaped with his own life by stumbling accidentally as he was led off to execution and collapsing on the ground. He was clubbed and bayonetted several times, but successfully shammed death. In the dead of night, he crawled away, broke the ropes which bound his wrists by rubbing them up and down against the cornerstone of a house and then, guided by a chattering brook, dragged himself towards the river. Here, he found two other survivors. After 36 more days and nights of hellish adventure, Lieutenant Hackney fell again into the hands of the Japanese, and was again savagely beaten up.

There are other tales of the beheading, in all, of about 200 Australian and Indian prisoners-of-war, following our grave military setbacks at Parit Sulong. (The sworn evidence of two sepoy survivors of this mass murder has been confirmed by the post-war discovery of the remains. The War Crimes Court, in 1950, sentenced General Nishimura to death for it).

Jemadar John Benedict, a Madras sapper, has a vivid memory of this time of horror (he won the Military Medal for his courage throughout it).

Marched, as a wounded man, to the riverside for execution, Benedict suddenly jumped into the stream and swam away under water while the Japs fired in vain. From under some fallen trees on the far bank, he watched the hideous massacre of the rest of our wounded. In the night, hearing a cry for help, he swam back across the river, where he found a couple of his comrades. One had his head half severed. Benedict somehow got them over the water, and for the next fortnight they tried to make their way back to the British lines, but they were captured again, and jailed. The Fourteenth Army freed these heroes in 1945.

So ended the Battle of Muar. Was it not possible for it to have ended differently? For example, could not the 53rd Brigade have re-captured from the Japanese raiding force both that defile beyond the causeway and the Parit Sulong bridge?

There seems to have been an almost incredible miscarriage of signals ordering the counter-attack on the very day that the defile was lost (19th January). Next day was taken up in mustering the requisite infantry and artillery, and on the third day (no doubt, having been thoroughly informed by the Jap wireless-equipped patrols in the area), the enemy aircraft flew in and bombed and machine-gunned our troops as they deployed for battle. For our failure to move faster, our shortage of signal equipment and transport must be blamed; for the exposure of our troops to air attack, our sad inferiority in aircraft strength. During the week in question, the Japs were able to operate 250 bombers and 150 fighters from air-fields in Malaya and South Siam. Allied aircraft available were probably two or three dozen bombers and about as many fighters.

The series of defeats suffered by our troops in the field may certainly be set down, above all, to their lack of training. Thus, General Percival has said of the 45th Indian Brigade:

'This Brigade had never been fit for employment in a
theatre of war. It was not that there was anything wrong
with the raw material, but simply it was raw.'[1]

But one vitally important thing had been achieved by this
Brigade's dogged if foredoomed resistance in nearly a week
of night–and–day battle. While they fought on from Muar
Harbour to Parit Sulong bridge, holding up a crack division
of the Japanese Imperial Guards strongly backed by air and
tank support, the three brigades of 'Westforce' in the Segamat area were enabled to withdraw safely down the central
trunk road to Labis, and thence towards the key crossways at
Yong Peng.

Now the 45th Indian Brigade itself no longer existed. So
shattering, indeed, had been its losses, especially in officers,
that it was never possible to rebuild the unit during the few
remaining weeks of the campaign in Malaya. A fitting tribute,
both to his own outstanding valour and also to the service
and self-sacrifice of his men, was the award of the Victoria
Cross to the last Commander of the Brigade, Lt.-Col. C. G.
Anderson.

The bloody Battle of Muar passed into history at noon,
22nd January. Already, the shadows were closing in upon
Singapore.

---

[1] In his *Despatches.* See above.

CHAPTER TEN

LAST STEPS TO SINGAPORE

B Y this time it had dawned upon High Authority in London
that the Battle of Singapore was now near at hand—and
that neither its duration was likely to be very long nor its
outcome very happy for our cause.

This enlightenment had come after an exchange of telegrams between General Wavell, as Supreme Commander of
A.B.D.A., and Mr Winston Churchill, the Prime Minister.

It was on 15th January that Churchill (who was then still
on his visit to President Roosevelt in Washington) cabled
Wavell, asking him what would happen in the event of the
British Forces in Malaya being compelled to withdraw from
the mainland into Singapore Island? What defences existed
in the landward side, could the 'Fortress cannon' command
the Johore Straits, was everything prepared, and what about
evacuating the 'useless mouths,' etc., etc.? For, said
Churchill:

> 'It has always seemed to me that the vital need is to
> prolong the defence of the Island to the last possible
> minute, but of course I hope it will not come to this.'[1]

He was rudely shocked to read (on his return to London,
19th January) Wavell's reply. It said:

> 'Until quite recently all plans were based on repulsing
> seaborne attacks on the Island and holding land attack

[1] *The Second World War*. Vol. IV. By Winston Churchill.

in Johore or farther North, and little or nothing was done
to construct defences on North side of Island to prevent
crossing Johore Straits, though arrangements had been
made to blow up the Causeway.'[1]

In his vivid history of the Second World War, Winston
Churchill has told us what he violently felt (and still feels!)
about this astonishing information.[2] To the Chiefs of Staff
Committee in Whitehall that same day he sent a vehement
minute:

'I must confess to being staggered by Wavell's telegram
of the 15th and other telegrams on the same subject. It
never occurred to me for a moment, nor to Sir John Dill,
with whom I discussed the matter on the outward voyage,
that the gorge of the fortress of Singapore, with its splendid moat half-a-mile wide, was not entirely fortified
against an attack from the northward. What is the use
of having an island for a fortress if it is not to be made
into a citadel?

To construct a line of detached works, with searchlights
and cross-fire combined with immense wiring and
obstruction of the swamp area, and to provide the proper ammunition to enable the fortress guns to dominate
enemy batteries planted in Johore, was an elementary

[1] *Ibid.*

[2] *The Second World War.* Vol. IV. By Winston Churchill.
Churchill writes of his:
'feelings of painful surprise. . . So there were no permanent fortifications
covering the landward side of the Naval Base and of the city! Moreover, even
more astounding, no measures worth speaking of had been taken by any of
the commanders since the war began, and more especially since the Japanese
had established themselves in Indo-China, to construct field defences. They
had not even mentioned the fact they did not exist . . . it had never entered into
my head that no circle of detached forts of a permanent character protected
the rear of the famous fortress. I cannot understand how it was that I did not
know this. But none of the officers on the spot and none of my professional
advisers at home seem to have realised this awful need. . . .
I do not write this in any way to excuse myself. I ought to have known. My
advisers ought to have known and I ought to have been told, and I ought to
have asked. The reason I had not asked about this matter, amid the thousands
of questions I put, was that the possibility of Singapore having no landward
defences no more entered into my mind than that of a battleship being
launched without a bottom.'

peace-time provision which it is incredible did not exist
in a fortress which has been twenty years building.'[1]

Re-emphasising that 'seaward batteries and a Naval Base
do not constitute a fortress, which is a *completely encircled*
strong place,' Churchill pointed out that as things were, this
fabled Fortress Singapore lay at the mercy of 10,000 resolute
enemy raiders, crossing the Johore Straits in small boats. He
added:

> 'I warn you this will be one of the greatest scandals that
> could possibly be exposed.'[2]

And then, Churchill set forth a Ten-Point Plan for a really
determined defence of Singapore 'to the death.' This included
the effective use of existing fortress artillery on the northern
shores, the building of strong-points for field artillery and
machine-gun crossfire, the guarding and mining of possible
main landing-places, the wiring and the laying of booby-
traps in the more remote mangrove swamps, the taking-over
(or the destruction) of all small seacraft, the organising
of mobile counter-attack columns, and the mobilising
of the entire male population of the island for the con-
struction of defence works. ('The most rigorous compulsion
is to be used, up to the limit where picks and shovels are
available.')[3]

Orders to this effect went out to General Wavell next day
(20th January) from the Chiefs of Staff. They were accompanied by a personal message from the Prime Minister:

[1]*Ibid*

In fairness to 'the commanders . . . and officers on the spot' whom Churchill
castigates for not constructing more defences on Singapore Island, it must be
pointed out that while these men could make recommendations to the Committee of Imperial Defence (before the war) or to the Chiefs of Staff Committee
(during the war), they had no authority—or finance—to embark on such
building without permission.

It should also be noted that the object laid down in the original Defence
Plan was the security of the Naval Base, not of Singapore Island. And as the
Base is on the North-eastern coastline, any effective defences would have to
be far up the mainland of Malaya. Author's note.

[2]*The Second World War*. Vol. IV. By Winston S. Churchill.

[3]*Ibid.*

'I want to make it absolutely clear that I expect every inch of ground to be defended, every scrap of material or defences to be blown to pieces to prevent capture by the enemy, and no question of surrender to be entertained until after protracted fighting among the ruins of Singapore City.'[1]

Now all this sounds most clear-cut and resolute. But the reader should be warned that, in fact, a variety of conflicting interests beset Mr Churchill's mind at this time.[2] Thus, apart from the major strategic issue as to whether our main effort should be directed towards the war in Europe or the war in the Far East, there arose the question as to which was of primary importance in the struggle with Japan—to hold Malaya, or Burma?

The very day that the above-mentioned cable went off to Wavell, Churchill was writing to the Chiefs of Staff

'Obviously nothing should distract us from the Battle of Singapore, but should Singapore fall quick transference of forces to Burma might be possible. As a strategic object, I regard keeping the Burma Road (to China) open as more important than the retention of Singapore.'[3]

When, first thing next morning, Churchill awoke to read a pessimistic message from Wavell warning him that if Johore fell then Singapore could not be held for long, he 'began to think more of Burma and of the reinforcements on the way to Singapore. These could be doomed or diverted.'

So, off to the Chiefs of Staff went another Churchillian memo. It asked what would be the particular value to the Japanese in capturing Singapore (if effective naval demolitions had already been carried out there), compared with occupying Burma and cutting our only line of land com-

---

[1] *Ibid.*
[2] The evidence of this is clearly set out by himself in his book, *The Second World War*, Vol. IV, by Winston Churchill' Author's note.
[3] *Ibid.*

munication with the Chinese, whose troops had so far been the most successful fighters against the Japanese?

> 'We may, by muddling things and hesitating to take an ugly decision, lose *both* Singapore and the Burma Road,' wrote Churchill. 'Obviously the decision depends upon how long the defence of Singapore Island can be maintained. If it is only for a few weeks, it is certainly not worth losing all our reinforcements and aircraft.'[1]

But, as the Australian official history of the War in the Far East notes, Churchill and the Chiefs of Staff did hesitate to take the 'ugly decision' to divert the reinforcements then on their way to Singapore. Sir Earle Page, the Australian Minister in London, got hold of a copy of Churchill's memo and cabled it to Mr John Curtin, the Labour Prime Minister of Australia. A pretty hot protest came whizzing back to the Prime Minister of Britain.

> 'After all the assurances we have been given the evacuation of Singapore would be regarded here as an inexcusable betrayal. Singapore is a central fortress in the system of the Empire and local defence. We understood that it was to be made impregnable, and in any event it was to be capable of holding out for a prolonged period until the arrival of the main fleet.
> Even in an emergency, diversion of reinforcements should be to the Netherlands East Indies and not to Burma. Anything else would be deeply resented, and might force the Netherlands East Indies to make a separate peace.
> On the faith of the proposed flow of reinforcements, we have acted and carried out our part of the bargain. We expect you not to frustrate the whole purpose of evacuation.'[2]

---

[1]*Ibid.*
[2]*The Japanese Thrust*, by Lionel Wigmore (Australian War Memorial).

Whether or not it was this frank statement which decided events must be left to conjecture. Churchill says that it did not—but, at any rate, for good or ill, the reinforcements were not in the end diverted from Malaya.

Let us return to that scene. While the above Singapore—London—Canberra exchanges were going on, General Wavell had already (on 19th January) signalled General Percival that he must now work out plans (a) how to retreat, if needs must, from the Malayan mainland to Singapore Island, and (b) how to prolong resistance on the Island to the last hour. The following day, Wavell flew from Java to pay another visit to Singapore H.Q., where he discussed forthcoming operations with Percival.

On the civil side of the fence, too, things were stirring in Malaya. In reply to criticisms of the administration for the alleged slackness of their war effort, the Governor, Sir Shenton Thomas, issued the following to the Malayan Civil Service:

> 'The day of minute papers has gone. There must be no more passing of files from one department to another, and from one officer in a department to another. It is the duty of every officer to act, and if he feels the decision is beyond him he must go and get it. . . . In the great majority of cases, a decision can be taken or obtained after a brief conversation, by telephone or direct. The essential thing is speed in action. . . . Officers who show that they cannot take responsibility should be replaced by those who can. Seniority is of no account. . . .'[2]

On which the *Straits Times* tartly observed: 'The announcement is about two and a half years too late.'

The military outlook was not bright. To our setbacks in the western sector were now added sinister signs of enemy activity on the East Coast. Thus, as early as 14th January,

[1]See *The Japanese Thrust*, by Lionel Wigmore (Australian War Memorial: Canberra).

our patrols had seen Japanese troops strangely attired in
black coats and khaki shorts, with steel helmets, crossing a
river North of Endau. Within the next day or two, after the
bombing of the town and the decision to withdraw southward, there had flowed in reports of shallow draught junks
moving off-shore the port of Mersing. It became obvious that
a concerted air-land-sea onslaught was coming on the East
Coast, as it had already come on the West Coast.

It now seemed certain that we should have to fall back to
the 90-mile front of Mersing—Kluang—Batu Pahat. It also
appeared to be more than likely that pretty soon afterwards
we should have to evacuate entirely the State of Johore. The
formations covering these three named areas of it were
allocated their own separate lines of communication with
Singapore, and Percival arranged with their commanders
the method and timing of their withdrawal, should this
become necessary.

Thus, 'Eastforce' would retire from the Mersing area, via
Kota Tinggi, down the only road on that side of the mountain spine; 'Westforce' would move along the main highway
from Kluang; and the 11th Indian Division would go by the
coastal road on the Malacca Strait. All would then pass
through Johore Bahru, and cross the causeway to Singapore
Island. It must be pointed out that no prepared positions
yet existed on which we could possibly make a stand along
any one of these routes.

Even before the Battle of Muar had reached its fateful end,
the Japanese were closing in upon the Batu Pahat sector of
our new front.

Thus, already on 21st January enemy troops, almost certainly from that raiding force which had five days earlier
landed South of the town and occupied the lighthouse there
(see page 122), were cutting across both the coastal road and
the one that runs inland from Batu Pahat towards Kluang.
Indeed, they barely missed snapping up both General Heath
and General Key themselves, the Commanders of III Corps
and the 11th Indian Division, who were returning along the

Kluang road that afternoon from a visit to the Batu Pahat garrison.

The real danger of this garrison being encircled in the town had been appreciated, both by their Commander himself (Brigadier B. S. Challen) and by General Heath. Indeed, at their discussion this very day, Challen had urged that his force would be better placed to protect both the inland and the coastal road if it were withdrawn to a point East of the town, where the actual juncture was. But Heath had insisted that the town itself be held, and gave orders that it should be stocked at once with ten days' supplies. Frankly, he believed that Batu Pahat might be turned into another 'Tobruk,' pinning down the enemy by threatening his advance along the main highway. That same evening, the Japs threw a block across the inland road.

Batu Pahat itself is a small river port, rather resembling Muar, except that it is several miles inland from the coast. Here, too, is a motor ferry, with roads radiating from it to the North, South, East and West of the town.

Rising from the southern bank of the Batu Pahat River, are the forest slopes of the hill called Bukit Banang. Before the war, this district (like some others in Malaya) had been thoroughly well-prepared (in more senses than one) by the Japanese, who had bought and developed rubber estates and iron ore mines there, and had built up local communities friendly to the Japanese themselves. One of the former Japanese residents, indeed, returned to Batu Pahat this fateful January, 1942, as a colonel commanding an enemy infantry regiment.

The day after General Heath's narrow escape on the Kluang road, a joint attack there by troops of the Batu Pahat garrison and the 5th Norfolk Regiment operating from the 'Westforce' sector broke open the road-block and let a supply convoy through.

But by sunrise, 23rd January, the enemy was back again in a commanding position. When, later that morning, some British lorries on the coast road came

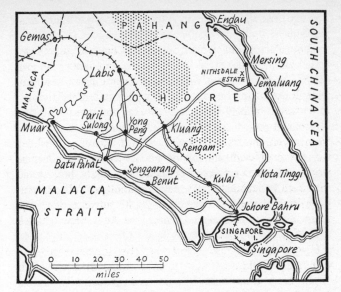

under fire, the complete encirclement of Batu Pahat appeared imminent.

At this point, Brigadier Challen's wireless link with 11th Division broke down. He made up his mind to get his force clear of the town before they were trapped there. The main body had already marched out when the wireless suddenly came alive again. The news of the retreat was reported to H.Q.—and the movement was at once cancelled by the express order of the Divisional Commander. The enemy had not yet occupied the town in strength, and that night Batu Pahat was once more in British hands.

Further inland, some misfortunes had befallen the 53rd Brigade as it tried to withdraw along the causeway towards Yong Peng. The timing of the bridge-blowing went wrong again, and many of our men were left stranded on the far side of the gap. The casualties were severe. They were perhaps more than offset by the losses which the Japanese suffered in the fighting a few miles further East, around Kluang.

Here, the last aerodrome on the mainland was in danger of capture by the enemy before we could destroy its buildings, machinery and oil stocks. A general counter-attack was ordered, with the 5/11th Sikhs making a flanking approach. Then, the main assault was cancelled. But, in the meantime, the Sikhs duly arrived on the scene and entered battle.

Hastily signalled from Brigade H.Q. to break off action and withdraw, the Sikh Battalion Commander took the most resolute course; he led his men forward at once in a bayonet charge which drove the Japanese helter-skelter from the field, leaving upon it hundreds of their dead and dying. On the night of 23rd January, all necessary demolitions, the destruction of stocks and the wrecking of the runways of Kluang aerodrome were completed. For a week or two, anyway, the Japanese Air Force had been denied jumping-off ground for Singapore.

True, we had also taken it away from ourselves. But by this time, we had already been compelled to shift our bombers to a base in the island of Sumatra, reserving the four airfields of Singapore Island for our fighter squadrons. These were now needed every day—and often several times a day—to meet the air raids upon Singapore City, the Naval Base, docks and airfields by enemy planes numbering from one to three waves of bombers, each in a V formation of 27 machines, and escorted by as many fighters. Our own fighters were, of course, also required to act as escort to the incoming sea convoys which were now bringing Army reinforcements to Malaya from other parts of the Commonwealth.

More of these desperately-needed units had come in from India on 22nd January. They included the 44th Indian Infantry Brigade (a sister brigade to that foredoomed 45th which had died at the Battle of Muar) and 7,000 Indian reinforcements. Unhappily, the 44th Brigade was equally raw and inexperienced. General Percival has told us:

'I dared not send it into action at once on the mainland, so I decided to retain it on Singapore Island in the hope that it would get a chance of some training and also be able to work on the defences.'[1]

The 7,000 Indian reinforcements were also almost entirely made up of young and half-trained recruits, with very few non-commissioned officers of that type which were the superb backbone of the old Indian Army. So, the greater number of these several thousands of soldiers (altogether, nearly the bayonet strength of a division) also had to be drafted to training camps instead of being sent to the front.

Two days later, 24th January, arrived the 2/4th Australian Machine-Gun Battalion and about 2,000 Australian reinforcements. The machine-gunners were thoroughly efficient soldiers, and went to work at once preparing defence positions on the landward shore of the Island. The others were less useful than the Indian lads, for they included those recruits of a fortnight's training.

Altogether, a truly remarkable *reinforcement* of the strength of this battered Army of Malaya—and within ten days of Winston Churchill's warning to Wavell about 'useless mouths'! It would have been better, indeed, for all concerned if these two convoys had never set sail for Singapore.

On the front, events had taken a further turn for the worse.

From the moment that the 15th Brigade re-occupied Batu Pahat, the enemy pressure on the town had been building up. Against this, manpower support for the garrison had come from the 5th Norfolks, who had been switched there by road transport along the coast after their failure to break through the Japanese road-block on the eastern side of the town.

But, alas! They arrived without the supply lorries which had been expected to accompany them, and now the shortage of ammunition was acute. It seemed quite plain to Brigadier Challen that the last chance of extricating his force from Batu Pahat was passing (the prospect of that place ever becoming 'another Tobruk' had already passed). He, there-

[1] In his book, see above.

fore, again sought leave from Divisional H.Q. to pull out. Again, it was refused. Two more battalions of the 53rd Brigade, together with artillery and armoured cars, were coming up the coast road to support him.

It was still morning, 25th January, when enemy ambush and road obstacles brought this to a halt. That afternoon General Percival himself, who had travelled from Singapore to the 'Westforce' H.Q., in a rubber plantation for another council of war, made the hard decision to abandon that 90-mile front from Batu Pahat via Kluang to Mersing, and to start the final stage of the general retreat from the mainland of Malaya. A little later, from General Heath, the commanders of the three main sector forces received detailed orders, maps and time-tables. That night, the British Army began to make its last steps to Singapore.

The trickiest trek was that of the 15th Brigade from Batu Pahat. Under covering fire from the gunboat, H.M.S. *Dragon-fly*, in the river mouth near the port, the rearguard of the garrison were clear of the area before grey light next morning. But beyond the very next village, only about a dozen miles away, they ran against the Japanese sited in a commanding position on the causeway across the swamp land.

Successive attacks failed to dislodge them.

So did the column of artillery, armoured cars, carriers and lorried infantry organised by the 53rd Brigade and commanded by Major C. F. W. Banham, which tried to break through from the South. It was ambushed and practically wiped out.

Three survivors were Banham himself, the carrier commander and its driver (both of the 3/16th Punjabis). They owed their escape to the extraordinary skill and daring—as well as the grand good luck—of Lance-Naik Naranjan Singh, the young man at the wheel. For he made the carrier leap the first Japanese road obstacle of wired tree trunks and tar barrels like a modern stock car racer, then hurtled through the ambush beyond and so onward to the British lines near Senggarang. At least five times more did he have to repeat his rodeo-riding act before the carrier toppled over the last road-block, and Major Banham was able to report. What he told of his journey convinced Brigadier Challen that there was already no hope of getting his own guns and transport any further down the coast road—and it was certain that the Japanese would multiply the obstacles every moment that remained before he could launch his next onslaught.

So as evening fell, the commander of the 15th Brigade destroyed all his wheeled equipment and artillery, left his wounded under the care of the Red Cross and the Rev. Captain Duckworth, a grand Padre, and organised the rest of his men into two groups to trek across country down the coast to the next British-held town of Benut, nearly 20 miles distant.

A last act of chivalry as darkness closed in upon this sad break-up was that of Flight-Lieut. Dane, of Malay Volunteer Air Force. Since the R.A.F. had no plane to spare for dropping medical supplies on Senggarang, he offered to make the flight in his little De Havilland Moth. And he did the needed job, tree-hopping just about a hundred feet above the jungle, so low that no Japanese fighter could dive on him. He earned the cheers of the survivors of the garrison.

That night, guided by an officer of the Malay Police Force along little-known tracks on the inland side of the enemy-occupied highway, wading through the mud and flood of the swamps and stumbling amongst the prickly undergrowth, the first group of about a thousand British and Indian soldiers trod their way towards Benut. They reached it late next day, ready to drop with weariness. A second group of perhaps twice as many, were even less lucky as they tried to move down the shore side of the road.

For here, one of the jungle rivers was too deep to ford. It was while scouting to find a way to get over, that Brigadier Challen fell into the hands of the enemy. His second-in-command led the group along the river bank towards the coast, hid them in some plantations and sent off his Brigade-Major by boat to warn 11th Division H.Q. of what had happened. Somehow, he slipped past the Jap sea patrols, and reported the grim news.

There was only one thing to be done, and Malaya High Command with praiseworthy speed and resolution ordered it. The remnants of the 15th Brigade would be evacuated by sea.

It was not easy. The seas were shallow and the shore was sludge. No good charts were available, and the job had to be done under the curtain of night. Few suitable craft existed, and no crews had been trained in the operation.

But after dark on 28th January, the two gunboats, H.M.S. *Dragonfly* and *Scorpion*, towing a number of small craft, set off on this hazardous mission. On reaching their rendezvous, the gunboats stood off-shore and the boats sidled up the creeks. They landed some very much needed rations, but were unable to embark more than a few dozen men before day broke. But during the next three nights, about 2,700 men, the entire remainder of the force were safely brought off, Here was an operation which, as General Percival wrote:

> 'Reflected the greatest credit on all ranks of the Royal Navy engaged in it.'[1]

It must be added that on this occasion, for reasons best known to themselves, the Japanese did not massacre the wounded we left in Senggarang.

Now, what was happening all this time on the East Coast?

We have seen (Chapter Nine) that when the Australian 22nd Brigade had withdrawn on 18th January, from the not-easily-defensible town of Endau to prepared positions in the Mersing area, the Japanese had been unusually dilatory in following them up. Thus, it was not until three days afterwards that they occupied the town, though during this time their patrols were certainly active several miles to the South.

It will be recalled that an enemy invasion by sea of this North-eastern Coast of Johore had long been expected. (On 15th January, our air photographic reconnaissance had

[1] In his *Despatches*. See above.

reported the arrival of a large convoy at Singora, which seemed destined for such an operation. In fact, however, the two divisions aboard were disembarked there and dispatched overland to mid-Malaya.)[1]

Early on 26th January, a considerable naval force was sighted about 20 miles beyond Endau. The actual strength of it was four cruisers, an aircraft carrier, six destroyers, two transports and a dozen auxiliary craft. Due to wireless jamming, our air reconnaissance signals never reached Air Headquarters, so that it was not until the plane landed at Singapore about 9.30 a.m. that our striking forces were alerted.

And what did these now amount to? A total of 36, and of these the antiquated Vildebeeste torpedo-bombers had only returned in the early hours of that morning from attacking Japanese concentrations on the 'Westforce' front, and had neither re-fuelled nor re-armed. It was not until past midday that the first flight took off. It consisted of 12 Vildebeestes and nine Hudsons, with an escort of 15 Buffaloes and eight Hurricanes. Meantime, our Bomber Headquarters in Sumatra were ordered to despatch all available planes to Endau.

The Japanese had already made a main landing there when our air striking force arrived on the scene. Because of the time-lapse, we had reckoned that this would be so and that, therefore, the enemy transports would be lying inshore in shallow water. So the Vildebeestes had been loaded with ordinary bombs, instead of torpedoes with which their crews were infinitely more practised. As it was, they scored direct hits on both transports and on a cruiser, as well as on enemy troops in landing barges and on the beaches. Scores of Japanese naval Zero fighters swarmed around the Vildebeestes, shooting down five of them.

The second wave of our air attack was still more expensive, for we lost five more Vildebeestes out of nine, and two

[1]Japanese military archives show that they did have a plan to make an East coast landing early in January, but switched the troops originally selected for it to the main front.

Albacores out of three. Not much damage was done to the enemy, either by this attack or by a later one by Hudson bombers from Sumatra. But our own air striking force in Malaya had now been practically wiped out.

We fared no better at sea—and could hardly have hoped for it. For we sent up from Singapore two old destroyers, H.M.S. *Vampire* (she was Australian) and *Thanet*. They carried only three torpedoes apiece, and missed with the lot of them when they ran into four modern Japanese destroyers and a light cruiser. The *Thanet* was hit in the engine room and sunk; the *Vampire*, after a lively engagement in which she was, of course, overwhelmingly out-gunned, managed to break it off and return to Singapore.

The Japanese landing force wasted no time once they were ashore at Endau. That very same night they were marching on Mersing by the East Coast road, pursuing, as it were, the 2/18th Australian Battalion who were the rearguard of the retiring 'Eastforce.'

If the Japs despaired, however, of making contact with this enemy, this time they were due for a rough awakening. For the next night, 26/27th January, as they passed through the Nithsdale Estate, ten miles beyond Mersing, they entered a throughly well-prepared 'box' ambush, with rifle parties on either side of the road and field artillery firing along it. The leading Japanese battalion was practically annihilated, and the main column tumbled back in disorder towards Mersing. It was another example of what a really well-trained force could do to this invader.

But such forces in general we still fearfully lacked. Because of it, the West Coast road had been overrun and our position there was becoming desperate.   On 26th January, Percival had cabled Wavell, warning that with our depleted strength we could not hope to withstand much longer the enemy's ground pressure, 'combined with continuous and practically unopposed air activity.'[1] Another 24 hours, and he was sending this urgent personal message to him:

[1] Percival's *Despatches*.   See above.

'Very critical situation has developed. The enemy has
cut off and overrun majority of forces on West Coast. . . .
Unless we can stop him, it will be difficult to get our
columns on other roads back in time, especially if they
are both being pressed. In any case, it looks as if we
should not be able to hold Johore for more than another
three or four days . . . our total fighter strength now
reduced to nine, and difficulty of keeping airfields in
action.'

As Supreme Commander of A.B.D.A., Wavell replied at
once, giving Percival discretion to withdraw, when and as he
deemed fit, into Singapore Island.

We have noted that a programme and time-table of retreat
for the whole of the Army still on the Malayan mainland
('Eastforce,' 'Westforce' and the 11th Division) was already
in the hands of the responsible commanders. The operative
date was now fixed. The final evacuation of Johore would
take place on the night of 30th/31st January. The three forces
concerned would move in co-ordinated form down their
respective roads—and in the case of 'Westforce,' also the
main railway—to Johore Bahru. Here, both an outer and an
inner bridgehead had been organised, and through them the
three forces would pass in turn and then cross the causeway to
Singapore Island.

Two of these withdrawals went off pretty well according to
plan.

The first was that of 'Eastforce,' who, once they had shaken
off their Japanese harriers after that ambush reception for
them in the Nithsdale Estate, south of Mersing, moved along
at their own pace to the bridgehead, arriving there on 30th
January. The second was that of the 11th Division, on the
West Coast. Now, although both their 15th and their 53rd
Brigades had suffered some rough handling and severe losses,
they had fought their way out of the Jap traps almost to the
end of the western shore of the mainland. Their only remaining duty was to retire inland towards Johore Bahru, covering

the road from the coast until 'Westforce' could arrive there down the main road and railway.

It was upon this central sector of the front that the Japanese kept up an unremitting pressure, both on the ground and in the air. Here, the 9th Indian Division was retiring down the railway, while the 27th Australian Brigade moved along the roughly parallel highway. Unfortunately, for about 20 miles between the towns of Rengam and Kulai (where railway and highway link up), there is no road at all by the side of the railway. This meant that all the guns and transport of the 9th Division had to travel by a separate route—and that their only fire support would be the mortars which the infantrymen themselves shouldered. Likewise, all their wounded would have to be carried.

Maj.-Gen. A. E. Barstow, the Commander of the 9th Division, made the following dispositions for the retreat: The 22nd Indian Brigade was to provide the first rearguard astride the railway, holding on to a position there until the night of 28th January, then withdrawing through a similar defence line which would be held by the 8th Indian Brigade for the next two nights, and so on, alternatively. The danger was that, as there was a network of estate roads in this area, the very mobile Japs might be able to interpose themselves between the two defending brigades.

A couple of incidents assured this disaster.

The first was the blowing-up, contrary to orders, of a railway bridge and with it the railway telegraph line. Now, because all wireless sets had been sent off with the Divisional artillery and transport, this telegraph line was the only means of communication between the different units.

The other fateful event was when the 8th Brigade took up a supporting position much too far away from the 22nd Brigade. Before the night was out, the enemy had moved in between them.

General Barstow knew nothing of all this when, early next morning, he set off up the railway in a trolley car with a couple of his staff officers to confer with his Brigade leaders.

From the rearward one, he learned of the premature demolition of the bridge. He gave the necessary orders about it, then pressed on towards his forward Brigade. Finding the broken bridge still passable on foot, Barstow crossed and walked on along the railway line.

Then, suddenly, a burst of rifle fire! The three British officers leapt for cover, Barstow to the right down one side of the embankment, his two companions to the left down the other. Later, they tried to cross the railway line, but again came under fire. They never saw the General again, and it is now known that he was killed there. After an adventurous detour, the two staff officers got back to Divisional H.Q.

Also never to be seen again, as an entity, was the luckless 22nd Indian Brigade. Knowing nothing of the plight of its neighbouring unit (because of the utter breakdown of communications, though they were only about six miles apart), the 27th Australian Brigade on the main road fought a determined battle throughout that day, repelling with bayonet counter-attacks all efforts to outflank them. As the enemy reeled back in confusion, he pulled a new, and for the moment, an alarming Jap trick of using smoke bombs to cover his retreat (Our men thought, at first, that the pall of yellow fumes was gas—and, of course, we had no respirators. Though not in fact poisonous, the smoke caused severe coughing and watering of the eyes). That night, the Australians began a comparatively uninterrupted withdrawal.

The extraordinary isolation of the 22nd Indian Brigade from any sort of signal or message even from its own Divisional Headquarters continued. So Brigadier G. W. Painter, its commander, resolved to devise his own operation to make contact with the 8th Brigade.

Lacking enough ammunition, and anxious to avoid further casualties which could not be evacuated, he chose to try and travel across the jungle instead of launching a direct drive down the railway. For four days and nights, bowed under the weight of their wounded, the remnants of the Brigade staggered on, through the thickets of the forest and the marshland bogs, making about half-a-mile per hour. Malaria, dysentery and hookworm raged among these weakened men, and the leeches, ants and snakes made sleep a nightmare.

On 1st February, Painter yielded to the inevitable, and surrendered. About a hundred officers and men still somehow managed to sneak off, and made their way about a fortnight later by sampan or fishing boat or Royal Navy scout rescue craft to Singapore Island—just in time to be made captive again.

The loss of this one more brigade—and the lack of any available reserves to replace it in battle—compelled General Percival to speed the pace of the general flight from the mainland. The date of the last crossing of the causeway to Singapore Island was put forward by 24 hours. It was a narrow escape (for just another fortnight). Throughout the last hours of daylight and darkness, traffic poured down the roads to the causeway over the Johore Strait.

As we know now from study of the Japanese military records, the enemy was counting on a sudden, swift stab from the West Coast to seize the Johore Bahru bridgeheads before the evacuation could begin. This plan was defeated when, between nightfall of 30th January and 5.30 a.m. next morning, the whole of III Corps passed without any traffic hold-up through some much-feared bottlenecks in the streets of Johore Bahru. Bright moonlight helped it and, strangely, hardly a Japanese aircraft hindered it.

By 7 a.m. the two remaining pipers of the Argyll and Sutherland Highlanders were playing the Australians and the Gordons, troops of the outer bridgehead, over the causeway, to the tunes of 'Jennie's Black E'en' and 'Bonnets Over The Border.' An hour later there followed the Argylls themselves, last guard of the inner bridgehead, led by those same pipers, making the very last steps to Singapore to the skirl of 'Hielan' Laddie.'

As the skirl died away in the sunny morning, there sounded a clap of thunder. It was the Causeway, 1,100 yards long and 70 feet wide at the water line, with a giant lock and a steel road and railway bridge, going up in explosion. There followed a moment of silence, and then the roar of water pouring through a 70-foot gap.

Once more Singapore was a real island again.

But only just. For at low tide, the Causeway gaps were not more than four feet deep.

CHAPTER ELEVEN

THAT 'FORTRESS SINGAPORE'

THE Island of Singapore, now to become the battlefield of the Far East, is in some ways not unlike our Isle of Wight.

It is about the same size (26 miles at its widest, 15 at its deepest) and roughly similar in shape. There is a more hilly area in the centre of Singapore Island, and the Johore Strait which separates it from the mainland is much narrower at certain points than the Isle of Wight's Solent (West of the Causeway, it closes in to about 800 yards). Another difference is that a number of islets are strewn around Singapore Island.

The City of Singapore is situated on the South Coast, and stretches four miles or so along the water front to Keppel Harbour. The residential area covers several square miles, much of it on the rising ground North of the city Here dwelt most of the population of the island, for there are no other big towns though there are a couple of small ones. Before the Japanese invasion of Malaya, Singapore had numbered about half-a-million people. Now, in the New Year of 1942, the flood of refugees from up-country had practically doubled that figure. We shall deal, in a moment, with the grave problems which this created.

The Naval Base was built on the northern coast of Singapore Island, in that part of the Johore Strait which lies eastward of the Causeway and, being the widest part, is navigable for the largest ships afloat. Because the pre-war plans for the defence of 'Fortress Singapore' and the Naval Base were laid on the reckoning that the enemy attack would come from the East and seaward, the heavy guns had been sited to cover that direction and the arcs of fire of some did not extend all round. Moreover, by far the greater part of their ammunition was armour-piercing for use against warships. Unlike high explosive, these shells bury themselves deep into the ground before blowing up, so that their value against land targets is limited. As things happened, the beach defences of the Naval Base (and of Singapore City, too!) proved to be of even less benefit.

These defences began around Changi, which is at the easternmost point of the Island, and existed in the form of some concrete pill-boxes, anti-boat and anti-tank obstacles, gun posts, land mines and barbed-wire fences and traps. They stretched North-west up the Johore Strait to the Naval Base, and South-west down the seashore to beyond Singapore City. In fact, they covered the two main areas which the Japanese never attacked. The two areas where they *did* attack, in the North and in the West, and where General Wavell had for weeks previously pressed for something to be done, were left almost naked to the invader.

There were reasons for this.

An outstanding one was, once more, the desertion of civilian labour. Japanese air bombing and machine-gunning had already driven masses of Asiatic workers from the docks and factories; it was hardly likely that they could be recruited to do jobs on air strips or gun sites or defence positions which, in view of the enemy's now almost complete command of the skies, were even more likely slaughter-yards. Such work as was actually done can be credited almost entirely to Army sappers and companies organised from the reinforcement camps.

It is true, as General Percival has claimed, that by the time the Japs were ready to mount their assault on 'Fortress Singapore':

> 'Sites for forward defended localities and for reserves had been selected. Artillery observation posts and gun

positions had been reconnoitred and selected. Locations of formation Headquarters had been fixed and communications arranged. . . .'[1]

But it is also true that in many places very little actual building or digging had been done, even on main defence lines. Thus, in the western part of the island there is a natural strong point on the narrow ridge which rises above the sources of two rivers. One of these, the Kranji, flows North to the Johore Strait. The other, the Jurong, flows South to the ocean. Here, mapped and reconnoitred before the Japs first stormed into Malaya in December, 1941, was the so-called 'Jurong Line.' When, seven weeks later, the last British rearguard marched across the Causeway into Singapore Island, though a considerable amount of clearing had been done to provide fields of fire hardly an anti-tank ditch had been dug on the Jurong Line.

But even graver than the lack of labour to build defences, was the shortage of troops to man them. This problem, of course, was mixed with that of the actual geography of the Island.

Thus, the coastline is about 70 miles long, and if the nearby islets are to be taken into account, the distance amounts to nearly 80. Then, the northern and western shores are heavily intersected with rivers, creeks and swamps. Much of the island is covered by rubber and other plantations, and in the highland heart of it is a twelve square miles area of secondary jungle. To guard the lot, General Percival now mustered a garrison of approximately 85,000 men, of whom some 15,000 were base, administrative and non-combatant personnel; the remaining 70,000 included many serving in second-line combat units. It will be appreciated that if the whole of this lengthy possible front was to be covered it could only be done so pretty thinly. And with the enemy commanding the seas, of course, he would be able to launch his attack upon any sectors that he chose.

[1]See his book.

Two alternatives, therefore, offered themselves to Percival.

Either, he could try to prevent the Japs from landing in force, throwing back into the sea those who struggled ashore; **or**, he could simply patrol the coastline, holding back a strong, centralised force to strike at the invaders in a decisive inland battle. Because of the lack of depth in which to manoeuvre in front of the vital areas of the Island—the Naval Base, Singapore City, and the reservoirs which fed it—Percival resolved to adopt the first course, though he thoroughly realised its perils.

His practical plan was to divide the defences into three main areas, Northern, Western and Southern. There was also to be a Central Reserve Area, but this as we shall see was variable.

Northern Area extended from Changi right up the Johore Strait to the Causeway, and included the Naval Base and the two most northerly airfields of Seletar and Sembawang. Its garrison was III Indian Corps, consisting of the greater part of the freshly disembarked 18th British Division and the 11th Indian Division, strengthened by the remnants of the shattered 9th Indian Division. Lt.-Gen. Sir Lewis Heath commanded.

Western Area actually included the Causeway, and stretched away westward from there right around the rest of the Johore Strait to the mouth of the Jurong River on the South sea-coast. Roughly in the centre of the area was the Tengah Airfield. The garrison was the 8th Australian Division and another newly-arrived unit, the 44th Indian Brigade, and it was commanded by Maj.-Gen. Gordon Bennett.

Southern Area began next door at the mouth of the Jurong River and ran via Singapore and its adjoining Kallang Airfield to Changi, thus completing the coastal chain. Besides including the fixed defences of the Singapore fortress, it also embraced the larger islets off the South and East Coasts. The 1st and 2nd Malayan Infantry Brigades and the Straits Settlements Volunteer Force made up the garrison, which came under the Fortress Commander, Maj.-Gen. Keith Simmons.

In the *Central Reserve Area* was the much depleted 12th Indian Brigade, led by Brigadier A. C. M. Paris. It had been General Percival's intention to hold the entire 18th Division in Command Reserve, but so heavy had been the losses of III Indian Corps in the retreat from Johore that they had to be reinforced in the Northern Area.

Within these main areas, were also located the administrative units belonging to each Command. Thus, many of them found themselves within actual range of the enemy artillery, and paid the price in casualties. Such of these 'office' units as possessed arms were made responsible for their own local defence. A surprising number took to the rifle and the spade with sudden interest. What a pity we waited so long to give them the chance in 'Fortress Singapore!'

There was one more Command grouping—the *Anti-Aircraft Defences*, under Brigadier A. Wildey. These defences were not excessive to cover a naval base, a great port, four airfields and an army of 85,000 men. In fact, they mustered about 150 guns, heavy and light, and one searchlight regiment. In the hurried evacuation of the mainland, most of the warning apparatus had been lost.

As for our aircraft, even before the end of January 1942, it had been decided to withdraw the lot, with the exception of a single squadron of fighters. This was because, three of the airfields—Seletah, Sembawang and Tengah—which had already been heavily bombed, were now coming under close artillery fire from Johore. Only Kallang Airfield, next door to Singapore City, remained free of this latest flail (it was subjected to an equal share of the bombing), and it was for this reason that the last British fighter squadron was based there.

General Percival himself had insistently urged that some kind of token air force should remain on the Island. Morale, both among the civilian population and the troops, was sinking to a dangerous level. With the departure of so much of our aircraft and the demolitions now beginning at the Naval Base, panic might well have been set off but for the retention

One of the last pictures of Singapore before it fell. The vast black pall of smoke billows up from the blazing oil dumps at the Naval Base, set on fire by the British in order to deny them to the enemy

The survivors of a Chinese family struggle to live on in the bomb-shattered ruin of their Singapore home

The bombing of Singapore. Civil Defence men fighting the fires near the harbour

of this one mixed squadron of Buffaloes and Hurricanes. They did a splendid job. Almost constantly airborne throughout the hours of daylight, they flew into wave after wave of the Jap bombers as these swept over Singapore, and they took a heavy toll of them.

It was this bombing, not so much of the docks and factories and crowded living quarters in the town as of the reservoirs in the uplands and of the water mains which led from them that built up the grimmest threat of all to beleaguered Singapore—that a million people there would suffer, and perhaps many scores of thousand perish, from lack of water.

For, before the outbreak of war in the Far East, Singapore Island's plantations, industries and dwellings had used up more than twenty-five million gallons of water per day, of which ten million came by pipeline across the Causeway from a reservoir on the mainland. The rest was supplied from three other reservoirs in a catchment area on the Island itself. Now, even after an abnormally dry season which left the water levels lower than usual, by drastic rationing it had been found possible to provide twice the number of customers (the vast new clientele being the refugees) with a necessary minimum—*but always allowing for no wastage*. The air bombing and long range artillery fire was going to change that.

Less worrying, for the moment, was the food problem, both for the Armed Forces and the civilian population. There was probably about a month's stock actually under Government control alone, most of it in Singapore City or on its outskirts.

But an ever-increasing anxiety was how to provide the urgently needed extra hospital accommodation. Already some 10,000 sick and wounded had been evacuated to Singapore from the Malayan mainland. The Alexandra Hospital (West of Singapore City) which handled British troops, and the Tyersall Park Hospital (North of the city) which handled Indian troops, had been for weeks past packed and overflowing. Temporary establishments to lend all possible aid had

F

been set up in the great Cathay Building, in official Service and Government quarters, in clubs and schools and churches. The General Hospital and the many smaller ones did their devoted best to cope with the mounting civilian casualties, which were already more than a thousand a day.

Says the fine official record of the British Army Medical Services in World War II:

> 'At the time when casualties were most numerous hospital accommodation for them was most scarce, for hospitals were bombed, burnt and destroyed. There was soon no place in the island where the wounded man could be safeguarded from further hurt, no place where he could feel at rest. The surgical team and the operating theatre shared the hazards of the machine-gun crew and the gunpit; the nursing orderly in the ward was alongside the rifleman in his trench. The congestion was such that the Red Cross could provide no protection, for if it flew over a hospital its shadow encroached on a battery site. The piped water supply of the hospitals quickly became utterly insufficient; water had to be carried to the wards in buckets, and in buckets the refuse and excrement had to be carried out. For the patient gravely hurt, there was no healing hope of evacuation; amid the noise of battle he breathed the anxiety and the hopelessness that tinctured the air, and waited for the coming of horror magnified by his stimulated imagination.'[1]

A word about the bravery and devotion of the nursing staff—and none has been better said than by General Gordon Bennett after a visit to the Australian hospital at Oldham Hall School:

> 'The nurses were cool and courageous throughout the shelling, neglecting their own safety to protect their patients. Those nurses are the nearest things to angels I

[1]*The Army Medical Services* by F. A. E. Crew, F.R.S. *Campaigns*, Vol. II. H.M. Stationery Office.

can imagine. They devote themselves wholeheartedly to their heavy task, frequently working continuously for over 24 hours to deal with a rush of casualties. They never complain, and always have a smile and a kindly word for our wounded and sick men.'[1]

Singapore was, already, a fearful hurly-burly. The enemy's unremitting bombing of the dockland destroyed three-quarters of the warehouses and most of the shoddy go-downs where the dock labourers lived, smashed up the quays and compelled the dispersal of the shipping in the harbours, so that many vessels had to be awkwardly loaded or unloaded at their moorings. Our own demolitions, organised as part of the general plan ordered by the Chiefs of Staff Committee in London to deny the enemy all useful material and equipment, added to the chaos.

The Naval Base presented a particularly desperate picture. The great floating dock was scuttled, the pumping machinery destroyed and the fortress guns (at any rate, those which pointed out to sea) dismantled. Still more disturbing to the minds of the public who learned about it was the evacuation of the whole of the naval and civilian dockyard staff, first to Singapore City, and then by sea to Ceylon. The story ran around that this was the beginning of a general 'British bunk,' for if that vitally important Naval Base was being destroyed by ourselves, what was the point of holding 'Fortress Singapore' any way?

It caused such feeling that Percival deemed it necessary to issue the following public statement to the Press:

'The Battle of Malaya has come to an end, and the Battle of Singapore has started. For nearly two months, our troops have fought an enemy on the mainland who has held the advantage of great air superiority and considerable freedom of movement by sea.

Our task has been both to impose losses on the enemy and to gain time to enable the forces of the Allies to be

[1]In his book.

concentrated for this struggle in the Far East. Today, we stand beleaguered in our island fortress.

In carrying out this task we want the help of every man and woman in the fortress. There is work for all to do. Any enemy who sets foot in the fortress must be dealt with immediately. The enemy within our gates must be ruthlessly weeded out. There must be no more loose talk and rumour-mongering. Our duty is clear. With firm resolve and fixed determination we shall win through.'[1]

It will be grasped that it was not easy at the same time as this proclamation of resolute defence and defiance to pursue too openly the necessary preparation for a programme of demolition and denial.

As General Percival pointed out to the Chiefs of Staff, he had been given two objectives: (1) To hold Singapore to the end, and (2) to carry out a thorough scorched earth operation. But, as he says:

'The fact is that you cannot fight and destroy simultaneously with 100 per cent efficiency in both.'

Percival's own plan was that, as far as the Armed Forces were concerned, the authority in command of any dump, depot or establishment would be held responsible for preparing and executing their own denial schemes. As regards civil installations, this was the business of the Director-General of Civil Defence, who had his own staff drawn from the Public Works Department.

The task of each was knotty.

The military dumps had been widely dispersed over the Island to evade air attack. The new danger was that they might be captured by land attack. The largest of them indeed, were not in Singapore City but in the centre of the Island. Thus, the main Army food depot was near Bukit Timah village, roughly midway on the road from Singapore City

[1]See his book.

to the Causeway, and destined soon to be the scene of the bloodiest clashes.

Worse still, some of the largest ammunition magazines had been sited on the northern side of the Island (to conform with that fateful plan to meet an attack on Singapore from the East), and as this area was already being bombarded from the Johore mainland, these now vitally-needed stocks were endangered. So, too, were several millions of gallons of oil and petrol which were stored near this coast.

Because of the chronic shortage of labour and the interference of enemy gun-fire, not a great deal of the ammunition was ever retrieved and it fell into Japanese hands shortly after their landing. Quite a volume of the oil was run to waste down the creeks and rivers. The Japs seem to have feared that we should use it to create a wall of fire along those parts of the coast where we expected invasion. (Why didn't we?)

The planned destruction of civil installations, machinery, railway engines, tin and rubber stocks and liquor brought its own special set of troubles. Much of this material was private property, and since the prospects of compensation at that time appeared remote, it will be appreciated that the owners felt no great enthusiasm for the idea. A lot of the preparatory work had to be done in secret.

There was, inevitably, in the short period in which these different public authorities had come into existence, both some considerable overlapping and some 'gapping,' of which the latter was perhaps the most serious.

The destruction of the Naval Base is an example.

We have noted that this lay in the Northern Area, which was garrisoned by III Corps, one of whose units was the 11th Indian Division. Now the elaborate project (it was officially listed as Scheme 'Q') was due to be carried out by the dockyard staff. But when these were suddenly evacuated to Singapore and Ceylon, Rear-Admiral E. G. Spooner, who was in charge of the Base, turned the task over to the chief Sapper officer of the 11th Indian Division, without even informing III Corps Headquarters, much less General Percival himself at

Malaya Command Headquarters. A rather bungled business was the sad outcome of this last minute switch on Scheme 'Q.'

Could this, and other mishaps, have been avoided if a closer co-ordination of topmost authority had been adopted? Thus, was it not possible for Percival, as military commander, to take over complete control, according to the historic custom in fortresses under siege? He gave some thought to it, but was put off by three considerations.

The first of these was that the civil Governor, Sir Shenton Thomas, was still in office as the King's representative, and on the scene. The second was that Percival felt that as he had no previous knowledge himself of the organisation, the actual working and the personalities in the various Government departments, to make a change-over at this late hour would be more likely to increase confusion than diminish it. Finally, he was already occupied most hours of the day and night in directing military operations. Of course, if the entire contingency had been foreseen weeks earlier the necessary arrangements might have been made to meet it.[1]

One deed of organisation, though sadly late, was effected in time to bear fruit in coming days.

This was the rapid expansion of a force of Chinese Irregulars who had already carried out some useful harassing raids upon the Japanese lines of communication on the mainland. Led by Lt.-Col. J. D. Dalley, of the Federated Malay States Police, and officially known as 'Dalforce' (their nickname was 'Dally's Desperadoes'), they were recruited from all classes of Chinese, from college teachers and undergraduates to labourers and rickshaw boys, and including both loyalists and communists.

---

[1]According to Gordon Bennett (see his book, *Why Singapore Fell*) at a depressing conference of military commanders discussing civil labour problems on 4th February, he proposed that a Military Adviser to the Governor be appointed, who should be the strong man behind the throne, one who would force the civil adminstration out of its peacetime groove. 'General Percival,' says Bennett, 'seemed impressed with the idea,' and after the conference asked him if he would undertake the job himself. Bennett later suggested that he should be made Military Governor (a post which Duff Cooper had once contemplated), but offered to accept the other appointment if the Civil Governor would agree to act under his orders. Nothing whatever came of it.

Indeed, for more than a year past, Col. Dalley had been urging the creation of a network of guerilla groups to hold in check any Japanese infiltration through the hills and forests of Malaya. His report, *Jungle Ambush Patrols*, had lain with Malaya Command from December 1940 until December 1941, when the Japs were nearing Singapore Island. Even then, Dalley's efforts to recruit officers from the Malayan Volunteers, the Police and the Civil Service were resisted. The strength of 'Dalforce' was around 3,000—and it could have been raised to ten times as many.

In the event, its members played their part in the forthcoming Battle of Singapore, and a greater one in the darker years of captivity beyond, when they became the heart of a resistance in Malaya which would grow steadily until the dawn broke in 1945.

By 5th February, the siege of Singapore City (as distinct from the Island) may be said to have been formally opened. This was done by shelling Government House, the gunfire coming from a Japanese battery in Johore with a 24,000 yards range. By now, of course, both the Northern and the Western Areas were under steady bombardment and any further work on the defences there had to be done under the screen of night. Our counter-fire was already limited to about 20 rounds per gun per day, for General Percival reckoned on a three months' siege.

This same day of 5th February, there fell a harder blow. The last British convoy to reach Singapore was coming in, bringing the remaining units of the 18th Division. There were four ships and they were sailing by night, of course, to elude the Japanese air patrol. The transport *Empress of Asia* fell astern as she passed the islands, about seven miles South-west of Singapore. In the early hours, Jap aircraft picked her up, and soon the dive-bombers were busy. Several direct hits were scored, fire broke out and, after blazing for hours, the *Empress of Asia* sank. Some acts of superb gallantry, especially by the hospital staff, marked this disaster, which was largely retrieved by the swift arrival of Royal Navy rescue vessels from Singapore, so that few lives were lost. But nearly all weapons and equipment went to the bottom of the sea.

In the next three days, enemy artillery fire against Singapore Island was sharply stepped-up. By far the greater part of it, however, was directed upon the Northern Area, i.e. that part which lies East of the Causeway. If this was designed to deceive the garrison as to where the awaited assault landing was coming in, it failed.

For our night patrols which crossed the Strait to the region of the Johore coast which is opposite, found no evidence of enemy troop concentration there. On the other hand, two patrols of the 22nd Australian Brigade which reconnoitred the mainland West of the Causeway which is opposite the Western Area, reported considerable movement there of motor transport on the roads and of men massing in the rubber plantations.

At daybreak, 8th February, a cloud of enemy planes swarmed over the forward infantry positions of the 22nd Australian Brigade, bombing and machine-gunning them for hours on end. Then, about noon, the Japanese artillery began to lay down a really massive barrage, covering the Australian entrenchments, headquarters and lines of communication, too.[1] A brief lull at sunset, and then it opened up again.

Night fell. The enemy guns still roared, and flashed.

Ten-thirty. Barges and landing craft loomed off-shore in the darkness.

The Battle of Singapore had begun.

[1]Casualties were light at A.I.F. Headquarters, though documents and files were blown up, burned and sent flying in all directions. General Bennett's reactions were typical (see diary entry in his book, *Why Singapore Fell*). 'Anyhow, a little less paper in this war will improve matters.'

CHAPTER TWELVE

THE FALL OF SINGAPORE

T HE fighting opened with misfortune for our arms.

The day-long air bombing and artillery bombardment, and perhaps most of all, the late-night mortar fire which the enemy developed from barges towed out after dark into the Johore Strait and moored there offshore, had pretty well smashed up the British field telephone service. Now, instructions had been passed from 22nd Australian Brigade Head-quarters that our beach searchlights were not to be exposed except by the direct order of unit commanders, lest they be spotted by the enemy and promptly destroyed by their fire. This order was never given—due, it is said, to the telephone failure—and so our searchlights never went into action to light up the enemy landings.

Nor did our artillery, until the Japanese assault troops had got a firm footing on Singapore Island. This, too, may have been because of the same breakdown of communications, for no calls ever reached the batteries to put down the defensive artillery fire which had been planned. It was only when a few of our very scarce infantry S.O.S. signals flashed in the night sky that our guns opened up. (By the way, even our limited ration of flare pistols and ammunition was further reduced because the cartridges, swollen by humidity, would not fit into the chambers). Why didn't we use our radio service?[1]

In any case, we were desperately short of enough artillery

[1] General Percival himself (in his book, see above) has remarked on this 'strange and unfortunate reluctance to use the wireless.' It has not yet, April 1960, been explained.

to cover the entire front now being attacked. This stretched from Kranji River, on the northern shore of Singapore Island, to Berih River, on the western shore, a distance of about nine miles.

The Japs, on the other hand, had plenty of guns. Even their landing-barges had mortars mounted on them, which poured forth a barrage as they moved inshore. Because these were set at a fixed elevation, at first their bombs fell into the sea. But this still served some purpose, for they set up a screen of spray and smoke until the barges reached the beaches, when the bombs fell upon our positions.

One flash of luck (or should we say, flare?) did come our way. This was when a Japanese barge caught fire. Aboard, was a cargo of explosive crackers (the Australians called them 'Jumping Jacks'), which greatly added to the blaze, and must have grimly swelled the total of enemy casualties in the area of this flaming target.

It was 10.45 p.m. when the first Japanese troops came ashore. They landed in the sector on the right of our front, which was held by the 2/20th Battalion of the 22nd Australian Brigade.

The great mass of them had been borne across the Johore Strait in special armoured landing-craft, each vessel carrying about 40 men. Though here, of course, as elsewhere, the Japs used a notable variety of seacraft. Thus, there were also collapsible boats, made of plywood, with rubber joints and built in two sections, which could be assembled by one man within a couple of minutes. Driven by a two-cylinder, 30-horse-power outboard motor, these boats could carry at least a dozen front-line troops with full battle gear, as well as their own crew. Roped together in threes, they could transport field artillery pieces. And, also, there were steel and timber pontoons, capable of carrying trucks and tanks.

Besides these ferried invaders, came the swimmers. They breasted their way across the Strait (at this point a good half-mile wide) holding their rifles and ammunition above their heads. Quite a number had compasses strapped on their

wrists to help them find their way, and had been thoroughly
briefed how to reach certain objectives—and people! For
the Japanese had long since organised and deployed their
Fifth Column on Singapore Island, just as they had made all
the necessary transport arrangements to bring these special
landing-craft by overland route, via the former Jap-managed
rubber estates, to embarkation points in Johore within three
days of the British withdrawal across the Strait.

Both in their initial assault and in successive ones, which
were made from much more vulnerable barges, the Japs paid
dearly for their ferrying.

Thus, half-a-dozen craft which tried to enter Berih River
were sunk in the estuary, and their occupants picked off before
they could even reach the shore. In other places, where sometimes several attempted landings in turn were repelled, a like
result might have been obtained if our machine-gunners had
not run out of ammunition. If only our field artillery had
possessed more ammunition, too (and guns!). If only . . .
But there were so many vital things lacking on our side in
the Battle of Singapore!

A powerful reinforcement of our combat strength was
actually available, though it was not used enough. This was
personal initiative in fighting the Japs at their own especial
game—that of interloping behind the enemy's lines.

Thus, on this very night of invasion, Lieutenant F. M.
Smyth and two other Australian soldiers of the 2/30th
Battalion crossed the Johore Strait from Singapore Island to
the mainland in a small boat to listen-in and observe as the
Japs mounted their attack. Having done their job, they were
sailing back when suddenly another boat loomed through the
shadows. Smyth thought that it might be an Australian patrol
boat, and called out. Next moment, his own craft had been
violently rammed. He leapt at once aboard the enemy's,
flung a hand grenade among the crew, then leapt back. The
Australians next capsized their boat, dived overboard and
swam for the shore. Smyth was wounded, and never
reached it.

It took the Japanese main invasion force about an hour to establish themselves firmly ashore. From this time onward they were bringing over from the Malayan mainland, almost uninterruptedly, as much reinforcement, artillery, ammunition, tanks and transport as their barges could ferry. This remarkable achievement goes to the credit of the Japanese High Command in Malaya, and especially to the two Japanese Divisions, the 18th and the 5th, who made the initial landings. Between them, they landed 13,000 troops on Singapore Island during that first night of 8/9th February, and 10,000 more soon after dawn.

Their fiercest attacks were delivered from the West, up the Murai River and the Sarimbun River, and converging on the village of Ama Keng, which stands upon the wooded slopes looking down on them (and also on the headwaters of those two bigger rivers, the Kranji and the Berih). In an hour, the enemy had driven wedges between the three Australian battalions on this front.

This possibility had been foreseen, and battalion perimeters into which each could retire, if necessary, had been selected. Now, near midnight, the orders to do so were issued. But in the mêlée of a night battle in thick country, things went wrong again.

Thus, most of the 2/20th Battalion managed to concentrate a couple of miles North of Ama Keng village. But one of its companies, receiving no orders, remained in position and was trapped there. The neighbouring battalion, the 2/18th, whose planned perimeter almost embraced the village, got so closely engaged with the enemy in the forward areas that only about half of them ever succeeded in breaking away and even moving towards it. A similar fate overtook the third battalion, the 2/19th, who held the left flank of the Australian Brigade. Finally, when the commander of the 2/20th decided next morning to link up with the remnants of the 2/18th in Ama Keng and make a united stand there together, he found the Japs already in possession of the village.

It was fortunate that soon after midnight, following a grim

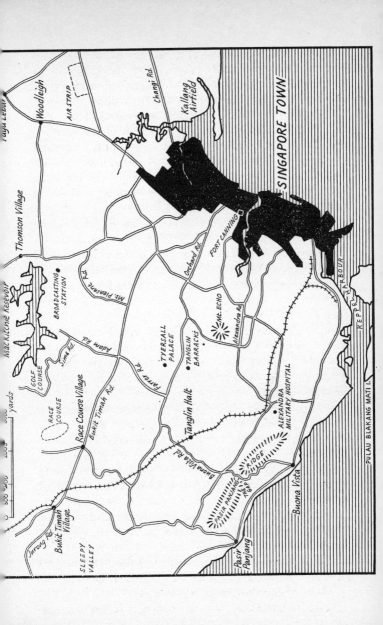

report by Brigadier Taylor to Western Area Headquarters, General Gordon Bennett had moved up infantry and machine-gun reinforcements to Tengah airfield, which lies South-east of Ama Keng and only a mile or so forward of that so-called (and still unfortified) 'Jurong Line.'[1] They arrived barely in time, soon after dawn of 9th February, for an hour or two later the Japanese were at the outskirts of the airfield. The Jind Infantry Battalion, one of the toughest fighting units of the Indian State Forces, who were already garrisoning the place, at once closed grips with them. The Japs were held there for the rest of that day.

They continued to move around the flanks of our position, and it was here that reinforcements were so badly needed. That morning, General Percival, as Army Commander, took a risk, wisely as it turned out. He sent forward to this area the only existing Command Reserve.

These were the troops of the 12th Indian Brigade, which after its hammering on the mainland consisted only of two sadly-thinned battalions. They were the 2nd Argyll and Sutherland Highlanders, now up to 400 strong (they had been joined by 150 Royal Marines, survivors from the *Prince of Wales* and the *Repulse* disaster, and were now known as the 'Plymouth Argylls'), and the 4/19th Hyderabads, 440 strong (of whom many were freshly-arrived replacements).

The risk was, of course, that the enemy would launch his main attack in some other area. General Percival, to some extent, insured himself for the moment by ordering Lt.-Gen. Heath, in command of the Northern Area, to put his own reserve, the 6/15th Brigade, at one hour's notice for general purposes.

That afternoon, Percival himself went up to Bukit Timah village, which is at the crossways of the main road from Singapore to the 'Jurong Line' and of the trunk road north to the Johore Causeway, to meet Gordon Bennett at his headquarters.

There, to the accompaniment of considerable enemy bomb-

[1]See Chapter XI.

ing and shelling, it was decided that Bennett's 27th Australian Brigade should still be responsible for holding the Johore Causeway in the North; that his 22nd Australian Brigade, with its later reinforcements, should try and stabilise the 'Jurong Line' in the West; and that the 44th Indian Brigade, which had been occupying a very extensive area in the South-west, from Berih River all the way round the coast to Jurong River, should close up so as to provide a much more firmly-knit flank guard South of the 'Jurong Line.' For enemy skirmishing and patrol activity, as well as what looked like a concentrated operation of dive-bombing, machine-gunning and low-flying reconnaissance, suggested that a new major thrust might be coming in hereabouts.

It was this possibility which decided Percival to move that absolutely last reserve, the 6/15th Brigade, to a site near Bukit Timah village on the actual boundary of Northern and Western Areas. They set off on the march that same evening. Final arrangements were also made for the destruction later that night of the oil depots at Kranji and the Woodlands, near the Causeway, and the effective sabotage of all remaining stores and equipment at the Naval Base.

This programme for immediate operations in the Western Area completed, Percival returned to his own headquarters at Sime Road to thrash out there with his staff a plan for another eventuality—a Japanese break through along the Bukit Timah Road towards Singapore City, and the neces-sary withdrawal of our troops from other parts of the island.

Once again, two choices presented themselves. They were these: should we fall back towards the eastern end of Singa-pore Island? Or should we try to hold a perimeter around the City? With the main military dumps, depots and crowded hospitals situated in the built-up area, Percival him-self had no doubts that it must be the second alternative.

So he drew up a plan to hold Singapore City, the next-door Kallang Airfield, the MacRitchie and Peirce reservoirs, and the hill points commanding the Bukit Timah region with its numerous parking yards. That same evening of 9th

February, he discussed it with General Heath (Northern Area) and General Keith Simmons (Southern Area and Singapore Fortress Command). Later, he put it into writing to them and to General Gordon Bennett (Western Area) as a 'Secret and Personal Instruction' to his three Senior Commanders and to his own Chief Staff Officers, in case events moved too rapidly for further orders to be issued.

As we shall see, this was to have unlooked-for consequences. (Such instructions are intended strictly for the recipient in person, and should be further communicated only to such members of his staff as it is absolutely necessary to consult. Gordon Bennett passed the instructions on in his own wording to all his senior commanders, some of whom failed to understand the intention of them).

It had, indeed, been a day of developments.

First, that enemy drive towards Ama Keng village and Tengah airfield, following the landings during the night on the North and West Coasts.

Next, that probing round the South Coast area for further possible inlets.

Third, considerable air operations. These had begun at dawn when, complying with Bennett's urgent call for maximum air support above the beach battle, our last ten Hurricanes on the island took off from Kallang to intercept a Japanese force of 84 planes, flying in from Johore. In two sorties, the Hurricanes shot down half-a-dozen of the enemy for the loss of one of their own (they flew back to Kallang halfway through the battle, hurriedly re-fuelled, then returned to it).

Air fights over the island went on for the rest of the day, and by nightfall it was plain that with the few machines we had left Kallang could not be used any longer as a base. With Percival's assent, the remaining Hurricanes were withdrawn to Sumatra, and Kallang became merely an advanced landing ground.[1]

---

[1] 'In the event,' wrote Percival (in his *Despatches*, see above), 'no British aircraft were seen again over Singapore.'

Fourth, as the day advanced, the Japanese artillery on the Johore mainland concentrated their fire on that sector of the Western Area between Kranji River and the Causeway. This was held by the 27th Australian Brigade. By 6 p.m. the field telephone cables had been cut and the defences around Kranji Pier demolished. A couple of hours later, in came the expected enemy assault. It did not go entirely according to plan, for some of the Japanese landing-craft sailing up the estuary of Kranji River got lost in the tributary streams and put their men ashore in mangrove swamps, waist-deep in mud, and with worse to come as the tide rose. Quite a large number of others, packed with troops of the crack 4th Guards Regiment, were sunk by our machine-gun and mortar fire. But by midnight, the invaders had established themselves on the Kranji peninsula.

Thus, within little more than 24 hours, the walls of 'Fortress Singapore' had been breached, and three enemy divisions were inside them.

Shortly after dark that night, we had sent three fast naval patrol boats (Fairmiles) on a raid up the western channel of the Johore Strait to sink enemy landing-craft and wreak all possible damage to his communications. They came under fire from both shores, but pressed on almost as far as the Causeway. They sank a few craft, then turned about and made a daring run for it again back down the channel, reaching Singapore safely. Another example of what more could have been done to harass the invader—and make more effective the defence.

A further one was provided by events arising out of a minor mishap. This befell Lieut. A. B. Watchorn, the Australian sapper officer of the 27th Brigade who was in charge of the blowing-up of the oil depot at Kranji. The truck bringing the explosives came under shell fire, and itself blew up. By the time that fresh charges had been collected, the Japs had advanced within earshot.

Swiftly and silently, Watchorn and his sabotage squad set their explosives. The valves of the oil tanks in the yard were then opened so that the oil could run to waste. As the black torrent poured out the charges blew up and set it aflame. Flowing out into the Strait, it met the incoming tide, which carried it up the Kranji River into the slimy swamps where so many Japs were still stranded. A lot of them burned to death in this flood of fire. (As we have noted[1], it was a Japanese expectation that we should deliberately set alight these oil stocks as a last-hour defensive operation. The accident at Kranji indicates its possibilities, though all would depend, of course, on catching the enemy just when the tide was running in the right direction).

Now fresh confusion arose in the Kranji-Causeway sector as regards military dispositions.

The landing of the Japs on the night of 8/9th February, in the region on the left bank of the Kranji River had already provided some anxieties to the 27th Australian Brigade, who occupied the region between Kranji and the Causeway on the right bank of that river, for it exposed their flank. The landing of the Japs on the following night near Kranji itself was much more alarming, for it opened up the possibility that they might strike across the Singapore-Causeway trunk road, which lay less than a mile away from them. This would not only have cut the 27th Brigade's own direct line of communication with the City, but would also have driven a wedge between them and the other two Australian brigades (12th and 22nd) in the Western Area.

Brigadier D. S. Maxwell, indeed, had made plans to pull out southward from Kranji and the Causeway to a position on the hill known as Bukit Mandai, overlooking the trunk road from the eastern side. He prepared this as early as the morning of 9th February, when he first learned of the initial Japanese irruption into Singapore Island.

General Bennett said No! But, by midnight, 9/10th February, the forward troops of the 27th Brigade had been ordered to withdraw. Brigadier Maxwell has since insisted that he received full permission from Western Area H.Q.

[1]See Chapter XI.

to do this, though it may well have been due to some swift changes in battalion commands that mistakes occurred. General Bennett denies giving permission.

At any rate, the brigade moved off. And so, the Johore Causeway was abandoned—and another highway to Singapore City thus handed to the Japanese. For, as we have seen, our own mining of the Causeway after the retreat from the mainland had been ineffective. At high tide, the break made by our sappers was enough to stop all traffic; but at low tide, men could easily wade across it. With the departure of the British guard on the Singapore Island side of the Causeway, the Japs naturally made terrific efforts to repair this vital bridgehead.

A grave military consequence of the overnight evacuation of the Causeway region was that it suddenly exposed at least two miles of the left flank of III Corps in the Northern Area. Neither Northern Area Headquarters, nor even Western Area Headquarters (who officially controlled the major operations of this 27th Australian Brigade), knew that they had marched out until after day had broken on 10th February. General Heath, commanding III Corps, was forced to make some hurried improvisations.

Meanwhile, near-chaos had descended upon the Western Area front, too.

Here, still determined to hold that 'Jurong Line' against all comers, General Bennett had ordered the 22nd Australian Brigade to contain the enemy in Bulim village, South of Tengah airfield, until early morning of 10th February. Then they were to fall back to a place in the Line between the 12th Brigade on their right and the 44th Brigade on their left.

But during the night, Bennett had sudden doubts as to whether or not the 44th Brigade themselves were going to get there in time from their rather widespread field on the South-west Coast. So he sent orders that they were to take up positions at the extreme South end of the Line, and their previously-allotted sector was to be occupied by the new Command Reserve, the 6/15th Brigade.

The switch was bad for both brigades. The 44th had actually arrived, and were settling in when they were told to shift out to a fresh and unreconnoitred place—and this time in the middle of the night! The 6/15th had also just reached their Reserve rendezvous near Bukit Timah when they got their own new marching orders to move on up to the Front. The soldiers' language in the British lines that night was as sultry as the Malayan climate in the day.

Next morning, 10th February, it was the turn of the 22nd Brigade to be in trouble.

It appears that Brigadier H. B. Taylor, receiving a copy of orders which General Bennett's Western Area Headquarters had based upon those 'Secret and Personal Instructions' sent by General Percival to his three Senior Field Officers (see page 174), mistook them for a direct command to retire at once to their positions in the proposed perimeter of Singapore City. A rather untidy withdrawal left a gap in the middle of the Jurong Line, which the Japs swiftly entered.

The remaining brigade on the Western Area front, which was the 12th, commanded by Brigadier Paris, did not escape their share of woe. They were now a much-mixed force, for as we have seen, an Australian battalion had joined up with his Plymouth Argylls'[1] and Hyderabadis. They had already been threatened on their right flank (the northernmost part of the Jurong Line), and now the enemy had been let in upon their left flank. Within a few hours, they could have been entirely surrounded—if they had not moved out in time.

Even so, as Brigadier Paris marched his brigade back towards Bukit Panjang village, through which the Singapore-Causeway trunk road passes, his patrols reported that they could make no contact at all with the 27th Australian Brigade, who were supposed to be linked with them on their right. The trunk road northward to the Causeway had apparently now become free-for-all, so that a determined Japanese drive

[1]See Argyll and Sutherland Highlanders and Royal Marines page 174.

down it might well have opened the gate to Singapore City itself.

To guard these approaches, Paris moved more of his men yet further back upon the village.

But this very action meant that the northern part of the Jurong Line was now abandoned—and unless the troops occupying the southern part of it likewise retired, they would find *their* flank exposed. Since by this time, their commanders had also received copies of those ill-fated G.H.Q. orders for a Singapore perimeter re-grouping (and had made the same mistaken assumption that they were to be immediately carried out), a general evacuation of the Jurong Line now began to take place. But with the breakdown of signal intercommunications, the movements of the various units were not co-ordinated and, soon, they became utterly out of control.

General Wavell, the Supreme Commander, had flown into Singapore from Java that morning. He got a startling picture of what was going on. With General Percival, he drove up to see Gordon Bennett at Western Area Headquarters, near Bukit Timah village. The Japanese Air Force were also paying the Australian commander a call that grey-clouded morning, and they heavily bombed the buildings occupied by his staff, though the bomb which made a direct hit on Bennett's own office failed to explode.

General Percival has a personal memory of that

> 'unedifying spectacle . . . of three General Officers going to ground under tables, or any other cover that was available.'[1]

In the event, none of the Generals or their staff were hit, though a shock of another kind awaited Wavell and Percival as they drove off from Western Area Headquarters. Then, suddenly there appeared on the road a mob of Indians, in army uniforms but filthy in appearance, bearing rifles but

[1]See his book.

moving in no kind of formation. Was this a deserter rabble, skipping from the battlefield?

No! A reinforcement camp had been ordered to move. The combatant units concerned had marched off with their own weapons, but a large store of rifles remained. The Quartermaster was not going to abandon them. He ordered his administrative staff to take one apiece, as well as their own kit, and to make their way to the next camp, for his transport had already gone. Their blackened clothing was due to the soot from the dense smoke-clouds sent billowing up by the burning oil stocks as we denied them to the invader.

Leaving Western Area, Wavell and Percival made their way to the North to see General Heath, commanding III Corps there. What they learned from him of that threat to the Singapore-Causeway road convinced them of the immediate need to set up an effective Reserve Force in the Bukit Timah region.

So, three battalions of the 18th British Division were detailed for this task. They were commanded by Lt.-Col. L. G. Thomas, and quickly became known as 'Tomforce.' One other firm order went out to the 27th Australian Brigade—to push forward and recover some of the ground which they had yielded during the previous night.

Returning to Western Area Headquarters early that afternoon, Wavell and Percival received a further jolt. While they had been on their travels, the enemy had made a fresh advance in the West and now the whole of the Jurong Line was lost. Indeed, Bukit Timah village itself, with well-stocked dumps and depots around it and near-by hills commanding a distant view of Singapore City, was coming under fire. On Wavell's insistence, a counter-attack was at once prepared, to be launched that same night.

The day's tale of trouble was far from ended. Before the two Generals had reached Command Headquarters at Singapore, the Japanese were closing in upon Bukit Timah. Fearing that the large petrol depot just behind the village would fall into their hands, Percival ordered it to be set alight. It blazed for the next 48 hours.

On the extreme southern sector of the front, stretching to the coast at Pasir Panjang, a collapse was only narrowly averted.

This occurred when an Indian battalion was violently attacked both on the ground and from the air as it marched to a new position. Something like panic started—and, worse still, it spread to neighbouring battalions. Men streamed in hordes to the sea. But there they halted (they could have turned towards Singapore), and were duly collected by their officers and marched back to the line. For some still unknown reason, the enemy failed to seize advantage of this unexpected break.

That evening, before he took off by flying-boat for Supreme Headquarters at Java, Wavell ordered the transfer forthwith of all remaining Air Force officers and men to the Dutch East Indies. By this time, indeed, our last airfield at Kallang was so pitted with bomb craters that it was no longer usable. But Wavell also told Percival that the Army was to fight on to the end, and that there was to be no question of surrender, and this was firmly (and even eloquently) set out in an Order of the Day which he issued.

Firmly (and eloquently), no doubt, because Wavell had that very afternoon received a cable from Mr Churchill on this same subject. Said Churchill:

> 'I think you ought to realise the way we view the situation in Singapore. It was reported to Cabinet by the C.I.G.S. (Chief of Imperial General Staff) that Percival has over 100,000 men, of whom 33,000 are British and 17,000 Australian. It is doubtful whether the Japanese have as many in the whole Malay Peninsula. . . . In these circumstances the defenders must greatly outnumber Japanese forces who have crossed the straits, and in a well-contested battle they should destroy them. There must at this stage be no thought of saving the troops or

sparing the population. The battle must be fought to the bitter end at all costs. The 18th Division has a chance to make its name in history. Commanders and senior officers should die with their troops. The honour of the British Empire and of the British Army is at stake. I rely on you to show no mercy to weakness in any form. With the Russians fighting as they are and the Americans so stubborn at Luzon, the whole reputation of our country and our race is involved. It is expected that every unit will be brought into close contact with the enemy and fight it out. . . .'[1]

The Australian official history of the war in the Far East has made its own pungent commentary on this. It states:

'Mr Churchill said nothing about the Malayan campaign being virtually lost at sea and in the air within a few days of its commencement; nothing about the disastrous dispersal of the army on the mainland to protect airfields now valuable only to the enemy; nothing about the Japanese monopoly of tanks; though indeed his figures did indicate that about half the force at Percival's disposal comprised Asian soldiers. These, in the main poorly trained and inexperienced, and with many officers who were more or less strangers to their units, were pitted against other Asians who had become veterans of campaigns in China and were fighting ardently for their country instead of as subject people. The United Kingdom troops included the newly-arrived 18th Division; more than half the total number of Australians, with a divisional organisation but only two brigades, consisted of other than front-line troops. . . . Singapore had been indeed a boasted fortress, but it was not the enemy who had been deceived by the boast. To Mr Churchill himself, as has been shown, it had become with a shock of discovery "the naked island".'[2]

---

[1] *The Second World War.* Vol. IV. By Winston Churchill.
[2] *The Japanese Thrust*, by Lionel Wigmore (Australian War Memorial).

Now General Wavell was off to the East Indies. One final blow—and a sharply personal one for the Supreme Commander. As he went down the quay steps in the black-out to board the launch which was taking him to the flying-boat in Singapore harbour, Wavell tripped and fell, injuring himself so seriously that on reaching Java he had to spend the next few days in bed. To Winston Churchill, the Prime Minister, he cabled this estimate of current events:

'Battle for Singapore is not going well. Japanese with their usual infiltration tactics are getting on much more rapidly than they should in the West of Island. I ordered Percival to stage counter-attack with all troops possible on that front. Morale of some troops is not good and none is as high as I should like to see. . . . Chief troubles are lack of sufficient training in some of reinforcing troops and inferiority complex which bold and skilful Japanese tactics and their command of the air have caused. Everything possible is being done to produce more offensive spirit and optimistic outlook. But I cannot pretend that these efforts have been entirely successful up to date. I have given the most categorical orders that there is to be no thought of surrender, and that all troops are to continue fighting to the end.'

Things had already taken a new, menacing turn.

As the day ended, a powerful Japanese attack came in upon the 12th Indian Brigade, disposed around Bukit Panjang village. The enemy infantry were closely supported by tanks, which were now making their first appearance in the fighting on Singapore Island. They smashed through the 4/19th Hyderabadis, who now broke up and disintegrated. The 2/29th Australian battalion held the Japs for an hour or two, but then were forced back into the hills on the East of the village.

This yielded the command of the crossroads to the enemy, who were now able to make the first real link-up of their separate invasions from the West and the North. The tanks then swung South towards Singapore, and though the Argylls (who were the only remnant of the 12th Brigade still in action) halted them at a couple of hastily-improvised road blocks, the delay was not for long and soon the Argylls themselves had been driven back on to the slopes beyond. The road to Singapore lay open.

The Japanese did not take it, though if they had done they would have been in town by breakfast-time.

The reason? In their own official versions, they say that their troops had reached their objectives and now had to wait for the supporting artillery and ammunition to catch up with them. The truth is more likely to be that they had not realised the extent of their own success, and the opportunity which it now presented.

For, further South, the ferment was far worse.

The counter-attack to recapture the Jurong Line which Wavell had ordered, and which Gordon Bennett had prepared on paper, had not the slightest prospect of ever being put into operation. The plan was for the 6/15th Indian and 22nd Australian Brigades in Western Area to advance in contact with the 12th Indian Brigade in three stages, and beginning at 6 p.m. on that night of 10th February, to be in full occupation of the Line within 24 hours.

It would have been an exacting enough task for fresh and thoroughly fit troops. To lay it upon men physically drained of their strength and, by this time, increasingly depressed in spirit, was too much. Added to the problem, was the inter-unit confusion caused by communications chaos, and by the fact that a great deal of the operation was to be carried out in the dark.

We have already seen what happened to the 12th Brigade. Before dawn of 11th February, it had broken up as a formation. The 6/15th Brigade lived on only a little longer. Attacked about 3 a.m. along the Jurong Road by the Japanese 18th Division, they held the enemy for several hours by a series of resolute bayonet charges. But as the 12th Brigade melted away on their right flank, the Japs poured in upon the rear of the 6/15th.

Unable now to move back along the Jurong Road to Bukit Timah, the Commanding Officer (Colonel J. B. Coates) split his force into three columns—British, Australian and Indian—and set them off on a compass-bearing towards the Singapore perimeter. As they crossed the Sleepy Valley, West of Racecourse Village, they fell into an ambush and suffered heavily in dead and wounded. Only about a quarter of them got through to the next-door unit on their left, the 22nd Brigade.

This brigade had not escaped unscathed, either. Its flanks likewise uncovered by the withdrawal of their neighbours, these troops had also been compelled to move out—and they, too, were ambushed on the way. Indeed, when they reached their new position near the perimeter, even their Headquarters were attacked by roving Jap patrols who were only driven off after a hard struggle, and not before we had found it necessary to blow up our 15-inch battery there lest the enemy should seize it.

Northward, our fortunes were in hardly better shape than westward. The same kind of confusion occurred about orders, and the same sort of gaps existed on the front.

Early on 11th February, General Percival discovered that we had no troops at all posted in the district, about a mile-and-a-half wide, between the Singapore-Causeway road and the MacRitchie Reservoir, over which both the Race-course and the Golf-course spread. Hastily, a composite force of a couple of battalions from the reinforcement camps was rushed there. Later that day, a second such contingent, under Brigadier T. H. Massy-Beresford, to be known as 'Massy Force,' was ordered to cover the approaches from the North towards Thomson Village and the Woodleigh pumping station.

Further up the main Singapore-Causeway road, a determined effort was made during the morning by 'Tomforce' (see above) to recapture Bukit Timah village and then press on to the next lost crossways, Bukit Panjang village. It was held up at the first village when the Japs flung two regiments into the battle, backed with intense machine-gun, mortar and artillery fire, and followed by dive-bombing.

So, the projected attack on the second village never materialised. There still remains a mystery as to whether or not it was to have been supported by a thrust from the North, delivered by the 27th Australian Brigade, who for the last day or so had been posted on the hillsides of Bukit Mandai, guarding the left flank of III Corps.

Indeed, it appears that until a very late hour, the Brigade was committed to the attack ordered by III Corps Head-quarters upon a third, and still more northerly village, Mandai. That operation had not succeeded because of orders never received, or else delayed, or distorted. Much disorder was due to the repeated switching of formations from one command to another. (Could it not have been avoided?) With the failure of inter-communications, as well as those between each unit and Headquarters, the trouble was bound to mount.

In the Northern Area, with the departure of the 27th Brigade from his left flank, the Commander, General Heath, had to make up his mind to abandon the Naval Base. Final demolitions were ordered, and by evening the 11th Division had withdrawn as far as Sembawang airfield. If they were to escape encirclement, it was plain that they would have to keep on marching, and all that night they did.

Another evacuation, on the whole a happier one, was going on at this time. It had been decided to send away from Singapore the female nursing staffs of the military hospitals, and 11th February saw the largest embarkation. This was aboard the cargo steamer *Empire Star*. She had accommodation for 16 passengers, and 2,154 persons, mostly Australian, Indian and British nurses, were crammed into her. Though viciously attacked by Jap planes, she safely arrived at Batavia on 14th February and then set sail for

Fremantle. Two other ships loaded with patients and nurses also escaped.

A terrible exception was that of the *Vyner Brooke*, which left Singapore the day after the *Empire Star*. Heavily bombed, she sank off Banka Island. Many of her 300 passengers (they were mostly women and children) were drowned. A more savage fate awaited some of the survivors who struggled ashore.

On Radji Beach, 22 nurses and 12 patients collected. A Jap patrol arrived, and separated the party into three groups, officers, men and nurses. The men were marched away for a few yards and shot. Then the officers were taken to the same spot and bayoneted. The nurses were ordered to walk back into the sea. When they were knee-deep in the water they were mown down by a machine-gun.

Back now to the hell of Singapore. A grim affair had sealed that dismal day of 11th February. This was the fire which broke out in the Indian Base Hospital at Tyersall, on the north-western border of Singapore City, following enemy bombing and shelling. The wards were in a hutted camp, and the flames blazed up so swiftly that only a few of the patients could be rescued in time. The lurid sky that night was a red warning of coming horror.

Thursday, 12th February, was ushered in by an early morning enemy tank attack thundering down the Bukit Timah road towards Racecourse Village. Held up by the steady fire of our anti-tank batteries, the Japanese infantry swarmed out from behind the tank squadrons and, by noon, had made serious infiltrations into the position held by 'Massy Force' ('Tomforce' had now linked up with it). Brigadier Massy-Beresford decided to haul back to a stronger defence line, which he had already prepared.

General Percival had also reached a decision—of a like kind though, of course, on a vaster scale. He reckoned that to try and still keep a grip on the northern and eastern beaches of Singapore Island, when it was likely that the Japanese would now make a major effort to break through to Singapore City itself down the channel of the Bukit Timah road, would be to gamble recklessly with his available manpower. The time had come, resolved Percival, to concentrate all remaining fighting power within a single military field. And so, back to that Perimeter!

That perimeter had by now greatly shrunk, for Bukit Timah with its depots and food and petrol dumps had already passed to the enemy. And General Percival now realised that if a close defence ring was to be erected around Singapore City, then the Changi district at the easternmost end of the Island, although it possessed its own well-built fixed defences and strong points, would have to be abandoned.

A swift tour of the front, and Percival was back at his new Headquarters in Fort Channing with his staff, drafting a plan. It was drawn to include both Kallang airfield and Paya Lebar airstrip, Thomson Village, the MacRitchie Reservoir, the Adam Road and the Farrer Road, Tanglin Halt, and the Buona Vista Road to the South Coast. It made a 28-mile perimeter.

General Percival then called to see Sir Shenton Thomas, Governor of the Straits Settlements. He was still on duty at Government House, though the place was under spasmodic enemy gunfire. Percival explained his plans, and both agreed that the Singapore Broadcasting Station, which was now within a mile of the front line, must be destroyed at once and thus be sure of being denied the enemy for any future radio propaganda. It was also arranged to burn the main part of the existing stock of currency notes held by the Treasury.

Throughout the day, the retreat to the perimeter went on in comparatively good order, though the Japs pressed hard with tanks and freshly-landed infantry and artillery reserves. They got at least three good hidings—on the road to Thomson Village, from British and Indian troops of the 11th Division; on the Bukit Timah road, from Australians of the 22nd Brigade; and on the South Coast road, from Malayans of the 1st Malaya Brigade.

But the enemy were not deterred by any sectional setback.

They had no reason to be disappointed, or depressed. They had allowed themselves one hundred days in which to seize all the mainland of Malaya and Singapore Island, too. It was still three days short of 70, and here they were, literally banging on the gate of Singapore City!

Friday, 13th February, dawned. What more awaited?

THE LAST STAND

THERE had been troubled hours, even before first light crept over the sky line on 13th February.

Disorder was now gathering within the confines of crowded Singapore City itself, where hungry stragglers wandered in, seeking their lost units—and where a dangerously-growing number of armed deserters skulked in cellars, or prowled the shattered streets in gangs intent on looting. Others were sneaking into ships about to sail for Java and Sumatra, or fighting their way aboard at the point of a gun, or stealing native fishing boats. Steadily, the morale of many units sank. More than two months—and more than four hundred miles —of ceaseless day and night retreat were now exacting their final pay-off.

The fighting spirit of some other troops stayed splendidly firm, including that of the very lightly-trained Singapore Volunteer Corps. Most of the enemy attack during this day of 13th February, was directed along the Pasir Panjang Ridge, to the West of Singapore, and astride the roads which flank it on either side. This sector was held by the 1st Malaya Brigade, who had given such fine account of themselves in yesterday's battle. In today's, they excelled their own standards.

Bombed, strafed, shelled and mortared for hours, then assaulted by a regiment of the crack Japanese 18th Division, the 1st Malaya Brigade held the enemy at bay until late in the evening when, outstripped in strength, they were compelled to yield the approach to Pasir Panjang Ridge known as

'Good-bye, Singapore!' One of the earlier, and more orderly, civilian evacuations from the port

Major-General D. M. Murray-Lyon talks with Major-General H. Gordon-Bennett

British prisoners-of-war in Changi Jail, Singapore, at the time of their release, September 1945

The Gap. Garrisons of their defence posts had been wiped out to a man.

That night, the remnants of this gallant force, with the 44th Indian Brigade on their right flank, fell back to a line stretching from Buona Vista village, on the South Coast to Mount Echo. This line was barely three miles from the centre of Singapore City, and just covered the key Alexandra area, West of the city, which included the British Military Hospital and our main ammunition and ordnance depots.

The need to safeguard the stocks which these depots contained was obvious, but they were not the only items now in short supply. There remained only one small petrol dump besides what was already in the vehicle tanks. Military food reserves were down to seven days, apart from those held in varying degrees by individual units. The civilian food stores were in not much better state, for heavy inroads had been made upon them by the influx of refugees which had so hugely swelled the population within the perimeter. Already lost to the enemy, of course, were several big 'secret' food dumps which had been set up in other parts of the Island, thus considerably cutting down the total available food supply. But the most desperate shortage of all was water.

The whole town area was now under artillery fire, and air bombing (with low flying machine-gunning) went on all round the clock. It is reckoned that civilian casualties had mounted to more than 2,000 killed per day, and the tally of the wounded and of those injured by collapsing buildings, or burned or blinded by flames and smoke in the blazing dockland hovels kept cruel pace with it. Then there was the water problem. Breaks in the mains were already far greater than repairs could be organised. The Director-General of Civil Defence sought help from the Royal Engineer units to reinforce the civil staff, and special water-carrying parties were organised.

There was no lack of rumours and alarms.

The radio installation which we had let the Japanese take

over almost intact at Penang poured out its day-and-night
torrent of propaganda lies about British Army secret evacuations, desertions and mutinies, and of civilian riots and up-
heavals. Oddly (or was it, for the final reaction suited the
enemy?), late on Thursday, 12th February, an exciting story
ran the rounds that the Americans had put ashore at Penang
a powerful 'Liberation Force' which, with naval and air
support, was going to fight its way through the Japanese to
Singapore. Spirits rose among the garrison of the 'Fortress'
—and fell even more sharply as no more news of this relief
came through.

Then, early on the morning of 13th February, came a
report that the Japs had landed on the island known as
Pulau Blakang Mati, due south of Keppel Harbour, Singapore. Communications had once more cracked up, and it was
some time before the facts could be established. They were
that this latter landing which had been made was not by
enemy invaders, but by British survivors of some of those
disastrous actions along the Jurong Line, who had somehow
managed to slip away by bamboo raft or sampan down the
Jurong River to the sea.

About three miles off Pulau Blakang Mati, there lies
another island called Pulau Bukum. Here were located the
Asiatic Petroleum Company's main reserves of oil and petrol.
The Navy was responsible for looking after them. Since there
was no further use for them on our part and they would be
invaluable to the enemy, Rear-Admiral E. J. Spooner, who
was in charge of operations for the denial of all Naval stores,
now sought and obtained leave to destroy them.

General Percival had hitherto resisted every such proposal
because he feared that the din of the explosion and the sight
of the black smoke clouds billowing up from the Island would
deepen the despair of the population and garrison of Singapore. Now, faced with the grim alternatives of destroying the
oil or yielding it to the Japanese, Percival agreed to the act
of destruction. It was put in hand that afternoon, but this
job was not well done, either.

Strictly in his own sphere as Rear-Admiral, Malaya, Spooner had arrived at another decision which, however justified, could not be expected to spread confidence. This was to sail away to Java that very night all the remaining small ships and sea-going craft in Singapore Harbour. There was about 50 of them, and with their crews, they could accommodate 3,000 passengers. It was the last chance of any organised evacuation from Singapore, and Spooner planned to share out the vacancies between the Services and the Civil Government.

There had been those earlier departures, marred by overcrowding and overloading, much boat-missing—and more than enough of boat-jumping, too! It was hoped that, this time, these mishaps could be avoided. As a fact, they were not. The mix-up (and back-up!) of gatherings on the dockside went on being frightful right up to the end, with armed deserters even forcing women down the gangways to make room for themselves.

The plans, however, were finally agreed at a conference summoned by General Percival at 2 p.m. that day in Fort Canning. It was attended by all Area and Divisional Commanders, as well as by the principal Staff Officers. Actual arrangements had already been completed by Admiral Spooner, unknown to General Percival, whose function now was simply to allocate the vacancies between the various Army formations and decide which types of trained officers and technicians would be most useful for future operations in Sumatra, Java and Burma—if they could be spared forthwith from Singapore. These were now selected.

But, absolutely No. 1 allocation of the available places, General Percival insisted, must go to the remaining women of the Military Nursing Service. This was because of the reports which had come in, telling of the savage raping of nurses by the Japanese soldiery after the fall of Hong Kong, the previous Christmas. (It was because of their bestial debaucheries there, that the Civil Denial scheme in Singapore had included—and had already disposed of—a million-and-a-half bottles of spirits and 60,000 gallons of *samsu*.[1] But, drunk or sober, General Percival wished to take no chances with the knights of *Bushido* when they might next have white women at their mercy. In the mêlée of those desperate hours it was tragic that some women lost their places aboard ship.)

What were the prospects that the Singapore perimeter could still be held? First of all, was it possible for the garrison to mount a counter-attack, and so relieve the pressure on the defences? Every one of the formation commanders agreed that the troops were so exhausted that such an attack would have no chance whatever of success. Indeed, both General Heath and General Bennett frankly advised an early surrender. General Percival himself did not yet despair, although he recognised that the situation was now terribly grave. He resolved to fight on still, and gave orders to that effect.

To General Wavell, the Supreme Commander, Percival sent a cable faithfully reporting the set-up and estimating that they could hold on in Singapore for probably not more than another day or two. He asked for fuller discretionary powers should capitulation then become inevitable, to avoid a full-scale storming of the town by the enemy, with all the subsequent horrors of murder, mass-torture and drunken sexual orgy which had disgraced those other Japanese triumphs. Wavell told him in a reply:

> 'You must continue to inflict maximum damage on enemy for as long as possible by house-to-house fighting if necessary. Your action in tying down enemy and inflicting casualties may have vital influence in other theatres. Fully appreciate your situation but continued action essential.'[2]

Percival also reported to Sir Shenton Thomas, Governor of the Straits Settlements, and the Head of such Civil Administration as remained in Malaya, the outcome of that afternoon's conference. To do so, he motored up to Government House, which he found empty though a sentry remained

[1] A Chinese whisky.
[2] See Wavell's *Despatches*, above.

on duty at the door. He told Percival that a shell had crashed into one of the cellar shelters, killing all of its occupants, and that the Governor himself and his wife (she was very ill, and on a sick-bed at the time) had moved to the Singapore Club, in the centre of the town.

As Percival drove back to his own Headquarters in Fort Canning to issue some further urgent instructions, he heard shots going off close to his car:

> 'Whether they were fired by Japanese infiltrations, or by fifth columnists, or whether they were only looters being shot, I do not know,' he writes[1]. 'It was all a bit weird and uncanny.'

There are many tales of civilian tragedies in these last grim days of the siege of Singapore. Captain D. H. James, an Australian ambulance officer, tells of driving along the Orchard Road this very afternoon when a stick of enemy bombs crashed on to a petrol station. It went up in a blaze, together with the nearby dwellings. Then came a horde of people, rushing or stumbling through the ruins. He pulled up near a house which had collapsed into the road:

> 'it looked like a caved-in slaughter house. Blood splashed what was left of the lower rooms; chunks of human beings—men, women and children—littered the place. Everywhere bits of steaming flesh, smouldering rags, clouds of dust—and the shrieks and groans of those who still survived.'

Further on, Captain James halted again when a frail Chinese woman offered him her little child. The mother herself was covered in blood and the child was also bleeding from a head wound. He cheered her up in her own language, and she smiled through her tears as his friends helped her into the ambulance car and attended to the child's wounds.

General Bennett himself had a poignant experience. As he drove back to his Headquarters from his conference with

[1] *The Rise and Fall of the Japanese Empire*, by D. H. James.

G*

General Percival, he came to an air raid shelter which had just been buried under the falling wall of the next-door building. A group of Chinese, Malays, Europeans and Australian soldiers were busy digging and shovelling away the debris. Then, out of the surviving part of the shelter came a Chinese boy, badly scratched and bleeding. He joined at once in the rescue work. 'My sister is in there' he said.

They toiled on, one wiry little old Chinese man going at it like a demon. At last, an opening to the buried part was made—and beneath was found a crushed pile of people, nearly all dead. Among them lay his wife and four children. He bowed.

That sweltering night, the 50 little ships sailed from Singapore. With them, aboard a naval patrol launch, went Rear-Admiral Spooner, accompanied by Air Vice-Marshal C. W. Pulford, who was Air Officer Commanding, Far East. A personal friend of Percival, Pulford had worked closely with him, co-ordinating as far as possible their two services. It was only now, when all Air Force personnel who could be spared had been evacuated, that Pulford himself consented to go— and he had to be shoved into it by Percival.

Nobody in Singapore seems to have known that the Japanese Fleet, in the form of Admiral Ozawa's squadron, was already cruising between the escaping ships and the ports to which they were bound. But the likelihood that they would be spotted by Japanese aircraft, and bombed and machine-gunned by them, had certainly been considered. So Spooner's idea was to sail under the cover of darkness, and to lie up in the shaded creeks during the daylight.

But soon after leaving Singapore, his launch ran upon a sandbank, and in getting her off one of the crew did painful injury to his arm. There was no doctor aboard, and so Spooner ordered full steam ahead, though the dawn was at hand. As they neared the Banka Strait, off Southern Sumatra, a Japanese destroyer picked them up and chased them.

Now, for the second time, the launch was beached, this time on an islet. A boatload of Japanese sailors followed them ashore, smashed the engines of the launch, and left them stranded there. And since all communication between them and their friends elsewhere had now broken down, they stayed on that barren mound in the tropical sea for the next two months. More than half of them died there of sickness or lack of food, including both the Rear-Admiral and the Air Vice-Marshal. The rest fell into the hands of the enemy a little later, and few survived.

A swifter fate was that of by far the greater number of their fellow-evacuees from beleaguered Singapore.

For they ran into both the Japanese Naval and Air forces as these concentrated for an attack on the last British stronghold in Southern Sumatra. The densely-packed little ships were raked with gunfire and machine-gun fire and straddled with bombs. Forty out of 50 that sailed from Singapore were sunk within a couple of days of their departure.

One of them, at any rate, took some return toll for this sea massacre. This was the *Li Wo*, an auxiliary patrol boat commanded by Lieutenant T. Wilkinson, R.N.R. She came in for her share of air attack, but was lucky to escape without any real damage. On the afternoon of 14th February, the *Li Wo* sighted a Japanese convoy, escorted by a cruiser and a destroyer. Though his armament consisted of a single (and not very up-to-date) 4-inch gun, Lieutenant Wilkinson at once resolved to close with them.

Now, though the troop transports were themselves armed, this was also comparatively lightly. Being nearest to them, it so happened that for the moment they screened the *Li Wo* from the far heavier guns of the warships. Therefore, though hard hit, the little launch was able to drive on at full speed ahead towards the convoy, and to ram the closest transport full amidships.

As she settled down into the sea, the Jap cruiser steamed round and blasted the *Li Wo* with a point blank bombardment. She sank with all hands. After the war, when the first news of this gallant action became known to us, Lieutenant Wilkinson was posthumously awarded the Victoria Cross.

Back in Singapore, the problems had multiplied. Over all, of course, were those directly due to the bombardment of the city by enemy aircraft and artillery. Many were the actual casualties, for the building of air raid shelters had been delayed until far too late (even the digging of slit trenches had been officially discouraged by the authorities— might let in the water, you know, from that sunken swamp on which Old Singapore was built! And even become the breeding ground of mosquitoes!) But affecting the physical and nervous condition of infinitely more people was the incessant scream and crash of bombs and shells, the alternating howls of the air raid sirens and the all-clear, and the clanging bells of the fire engines. For many a man, woman—yes, and child, sleep in this doomed city now came only through utter exhaustion.

Then, traffic—or rather, street-standstill, because of the mass of abandoned or smashed-up motor cars, trucks, trams and buses—jammed up in the bomb-cratered streets, with their debris of still smouldering bricks and woodwork, shattered shop window glass, twisted telegraph poles and tangled wires and cables. This frightful jumble further complicated the distribution of food, both to the resident population of Singapore and to the multitude of hungry refugee mouths, from the depots which had hurriedly been set up in large cinemas like the Capitol and the Pavilion to store flour, rice and tinned stuffs.

More urgent and most serious of all, since it affected *everyone*, military or civilian, was that water crisis.

Early on the morning of 14th February, the Municipal Water Engineer reported to the Director-General of Civil Defence that a complete failure of the supply service was very near. General Percival was at once informed, and about 10 a.m. called both these officers into conference, along with the Chairman of the Municipality. It appeared that because of the breaks in the mains more than half the supply from the reservoirs was now pouring away to waste. The Water Engineer reckoned that the rest might last for perhaps another

24 hours, or 48 hours at the very outside. (Actually within the next two hours the Japs had captured all the reservoirs on the Island. It remains another of the mysteries of this campaign why they did not at once switch off the entire flow.)

To deal with the present problem of almost overwhelming repair work, Percival undertook to provide sapper squads numbering altogether about a hundred men. But even these could not be put on the job at once, because all available Royal Engineer manpower was at that moment fighting as infantry in the line.

From this talk, Percival hurried off to the Singapore Club to see Sir Shenton Thomas, the Governor.

Sir Shenton warned of the peril of epidemic raging in the dockside slum-land if there was suddenly no water, and when Percival assured him that while he thoroughly appreciated his anxiety in this matter he still thought that Singapore could be held, Shenton Thomas sent off a cable of alarm to the Colonial Office in London. Percival's own message to Wavell, the Supreme Commander, brought back the reply that resistance must continue wherever there was enough water for the troops. Wavell added, later:

'Your gallant stand is serving a purpose and must be continued to limit of endurance.'

Almost as serious as the draining away of the water of Singapore was the now almost total disappearance of its civil labour. For this, the Government must be blamed equally for their failure to mobilise the military potential of the people of Malaya. Those labourers would have been as pricelessly valuable as the soldiers we missed. As things were, the smoking ruins of bombed buildings, the flooding filth in the craters, as well as many hundreds of dead bodies blocked the streets— and as every hour, this unburied pile of human flesh increased, the sour stench from it mingled with that already rising from the shattered sewers. To the sounds and the sights of defeat, were added the smells.

On the front, after a day of comparative quiet (except around Pasir Panjang), the battle had opened up on the morning of 14th February with violent enemy action in all sectors. Especially, did the 1st Malaya Brigade have to contend both with bombardment and infantry assault, and again distinguished themselves. But towards evening, when several hours of gruelling hand-to-hand fighting had failed to gain the Japs a foothold in our line, they brought up tanks in close support and at last succeeded in breaching it on the left flank. We had to fall back again.

There followed a military mishap—and a murderous horror.

The first was when the Alexandra ammunition magazine caught fire from enemy shelling, and our last reserves of the precious stuff began to blow up. The second was when the Japs entered the Alexandra Military Hospital. They insisted that they had been fired on by Indian troops from this position, and in reprisal bayonetted Medical Officers, orderlies and even some of the patients, including one who lay upon the operating table. Nearly two hundred more they crammed into a bungalow in the grounds, with standing-room only, for the whole of that steaming, sweating night to be taken out next morning, queued-up, and shot. *Bushido*.

The task of the 1st Malaya Brigade in defending this district might have been made easier—and even successful—if more co-operation had been forthcoming from their neighbours in the next sector. These were the various Australian units, which had now been re-united and were organised in a perimeter defence in the Tanglin Area.

General Gordon Bennett had that morning issued orders to them (unknown to Malaya Command Headquarters), that because of the shortage of ammunition, the Australian artillery were to fire only in defence of the Australian perimeter. Now, as this occupied rather higher ground than that to the southward where the Malaya Brigade were fighting, and so commanded a view of the approaches to the battlefield, much trouble might have been laid on for the enemy. Instead, the guns were silent.

This was not, indeed, the only example of the curious

behaviour of Gordon Bennett during these fateful last days of Singapore.

As he has since revealed,[1] he sent a cable to the Prime Minister of Australia announcing that if the other formations around him fell back and allowed the enemy to enter the city behind him, he proposed to surrender at once to avoid any more needless loss of life. Gordon Bennett did not acquaint Malaya Command Headquarters with this interesting information, either.

On the other, northern side of the Australian perimeter, were the British 18th Division, with all three brigades (53rd, 54th and 55th) fighting together for the first time in this campaign. Against them, the Japs delivered a trident attack, chiefly engaging the centre one, which was the 55th Brigade.

It was late afternoon before the enemy tanks broke through down the Sime Road, gaining perhaps a mile. They were halted in the gardens on the fringe of the Mount Pleasant residential area, but our own counter-attack to drive them back to their starting-point failed. Elsewhere, in this northern sector of the 18th Division's ground, we held pretty firm during the day's fighting and in the remaining, eastern part of the Singapore perimeter, defended by the 11th Indian Division, we hung on to every inch.

In the Woodleigh pumping station, on the North-eastern corner and within a few hundred yards of the Japs, the staff still stuck to their job. But by now, the damage to the mains and side-pipelines was such that five out of every six gallons were being wasted and only the low-lying districts of the town got any at all. But as Percival wound-up his long day of visits to the front, talks with Headquarters Staff and the Governor and the Civil Authorities, he had one last word with the Water Engineer.

'I think that things may be getting a bit better,' said that weary, but still cheerful official.

---

[1] In his book, *Why Singapore Fell*, by Lieut. General H. Gordon Bennett (Thacker & Co., Ltd., Bombay).

That night, General Percival slept a bit better. He was dog-tired, too. But Percival had not given up all hope, either.

———————

It was Sunday, 15th February. 'Black Sunday,' for so many a soldier of that ill-fated Army of Malaya, who would remember it as such for so many a miserable day. There had been some slaughterous in-fighting during the night, as well as an attempted Jap infiltration along the beaches at the end of the Eastern sector, which was dealt with by the 1st Manchester Regiment.

For Percival, the day began with a Communion Service at Fort Canning. He returned from it to receive the early report of the Water Engineer. It showed a grave worsening of the situation, which was re-affirmed a little later. This was at 9.30 a.m., when Percival called a conference of the Area and anti-aircraft Defence Commanders, together with the Director-General of Civil Defence and the Inspector-General of Police, Straits Settlements. It was the opinion of the Director-General that the water supply would not last beyond the next 24 hours, and that if it failed several days would pass before it could be restored.

Other items were in not much better state. The military food reserves were down to a few days, with the Civil reserves rather larger. There was a fair ration of small arms ammunition but very little for the field-guns, and almost none for the ack-ack guns. The only petrol was that in vehicle tanks.

What was to be done?

In Percival's view, nothing could be gained by simply remaining on the defensive. Apart from the water urgency, there was almost certainty that the enemy would take the city by storm—and follow it by a massacre or barbaric exploitation of the civilian population.[1] To the conference,

[1] As it was, besides the continuous torturing, mutilating and killing, both of prisoners-of-war and civilian captives, which was carried out by the Kempetai (the Japanese equivalent of the German Gestapo) throughout the war, at least two mass executions of Chinese took place shortly after the surrender of Singapore. One was on Changi beach, and the other one off-shore, the victims being taken out to sea in launches and then pushed overboard, to be machine-gunned in the water.

therefore, Percival posed two alternatives. Either (1) launch an immediate counter-attack to regain the reservoirs and the military food depots in the Bukit Timah region and drive the enemy's artillery off its commanding heights outside the town, or (2) capitulate. All present agreed that no counter-attack was possible. Grimly, General Percival bowed. It was surrender.

At this moment, reports came in to III Indian Corps Headquarters that during the night extensive Jap infiltration had been made into the sector held by the 11th Indian Division—and no reserves were now available to eject them. Also, on the other, western front, the Japs were forcing back the Loyal Regiment, of the 1st Malaya Brigade, to the very edge of the town.

As the conference rose, a telegram arrived from the Supreme Commander, General Wavell, urging that the battle be continued still if in any way possible—it ended:

> 'So long as you are in a position to inflict losses and damage to enemy and your troops are physically capable of doing so, you must fight on. Time gained and damage to enemy are of vital importance at this juncture. When you are fully satisfied that this is no longer possible I give you discretion to cease resistance. Before doing so all arms, equipment and transport of value to the enemy must of course be rendered useless. Also, just before final cessation of fighting, opportunity should be given to any determined bodies of men or individuals to try and effect escape by any means possible. They must be armed. Inform me of intentions. Whatever happens, I thank you and all troops for your gallant efforts of last few days.'

A deputation was now selected to go to Japanese Headquarters. It consisted of a senior Staff Officer, the Colonial Secretary and an interpreter. They set off in a motor car bearing a Union Jack and a white flag of truce on that wretched journey with which we began this story. A story itself of sadness, misfortune—yes, and of many a culpable mistake. But also of devotion to duty, of heroism and of self-sacrifice.

The men and women of this savage Battle of Malaya, the soldiers, sailors, airmen, the nurses, the civil servants and the police who stuck by to the end, were worthy of that precious flag which they treasured through those dark years. And we who were not there, salute it, may this never be forgotten.

INDEX

207

READ MORE IN PENGUIN

In every corner of the world, on every subject under the sun, Penguin represents quality and variety – the very best in publishing today.

For complete information about books available from Penguin – including Puffins, Penguin Classics and Arkana – and how to order them, write to us at the appropriate address below. Please note that for copyright reasons the selection of books varies from country to country.

In the United Kingdom: Please write to *Dept. EP, Penguin Books Ltd, Bath Road, Harmondsworth, West Drayton, Middlesex UB7 0DA*

In the United States: Please write to *Consumer Services, Penguin Putnam Inc., 405 Murray Hill Parkway, East Rutherford, New Jersey 07073-2136.* VISA and MasterCard holders call 1-800-631-8571 to order Penguin titles

In Canada: Please write to *Penguin Books Canada Ltd, 10 Alcorn Avenue, Suite 300, Toronto, Ontario M4V 3B2*

In Australia: Please write to *Penguin Books Australia Ltd, 487 Maroondah Highway, Ringwood, Victoria 3134*

In New Zealand: Please write to *Penguin Books (NZ) Ltd, Private Bag 102902, North Shore Mail Centre, Auckland 10*

In India: Please write to *Penguin Books India Pvt Ltd, 11 Community Centre, Panchsheel Park, New Delhi 110017*

In the Netherlands: Please write to *Penguin Books Netherlands bv, Postbus 3507, NL-1001 AH Amsterdam*

In Germany: Please write to *Penguin Books Deutschland GmbH, Metzlerstrasse 26, 60594 Frankfurt am Main*

In Spain: Please write to *Penguin Books S. A., Bravo Murillo 19, 1°B, 28015 Madrid*

In Italy: Please write to *Penguin Italia s.r.l., Via Vittorio Emanuele 45/a, 20094 Corsico, Milano*

In France: Please write to *Penguin France, 12, Rue Prosper Ferradou, 31700 Blagnac*

In Japan: Please write to *Penguin Books Japan Ltd, Iidabashi KM-Bldg, 2-23-9 Koraku, Bunkyo-Ku, Tokyo 112-0004*

In South Africa: Please write to *Penguin Books South Africa (Pty) Ltd, P.O. Box 751093, Gardenview, 2047 Johannesburg*

INSPECTION COPY REQUESTS

Lecturers in the United Kingdom and Ireland wishing to apply for inspection copies of Classic Penguin titles for student group adoptions are invited to apply to:

Inspection Copy Department
Penguin Press Marketing
80 Strand
LONDON
WC2R 0RL

Fax: 020 7010 6701

E-mail: academic@penguin.co.uk

Inspection copies may also be requested via our website at:
www.penguinclassics.com

Please include in your request the author, title and the ISBN of the book(s) in which you are interested, the name of the course on which the books will be used and the expected student numbers.

It is essential that you include with your request your title, first name, surname, position, department name, college or university address, telephone and fax numbers and your e-mail address.

Lecturers outside the United Kingdom and Ireland should address their applications to their local Penguin office.

Inspection copies are supplied at the discretion of Penguin Books

READ MORE IN PENGUIN

PENGUIN CLASSIC BIOGRAPHY

Highly readable and enjoyable biographies and autobiographies from leading biographers and auto-biographers. The series provides a vital background to the increasing interest in history, historical subjects and people who mattered. The periods and subjects covered include the Roman Empire, Tudor England, the English Civil Wars, the Victorian Era, and characters as diverse Joan of Arc, Jane Austen, Robert Burns and George Melly. Essential reading for everyone interested in the great figures of the past.

Published or forthcoming:

E. F. Benson	**As We Were**
Ernle Bradford	**Cleopatra**
David Cecil	**A Portrait of Jane Austen**
Roger Fulford	**Royal Dukes**
Christopher Hibbert	**Charles I**
	The Making of Charles Dickens
Christopher Hill	**God's Englishman: Oliver Cromwell**
Marion Johnson	**The Borgias**
James Lees-Milne	**Earls of Creation**
Edward Lucie-Smith	**Joan of Arc**
Philip Magnus	**Gladstone**
John Masters	**Casanova**
Elizabeth Mavor	**The Ladies of Llangollen**
Ian McIntyre	**Robert Burns**
George Melly	**Owning Up: The Trilogy**
Raymond Postgate	**That Devil Wilkes**
Peter Quennell	**Byron: The Years of Fame**
Lytton Strachey	**Queen Victoria**
	Elizabeth and Essex
Gaius Suetonius	**Lives of the Twelve Caesars**
	translated by Robert Graves
Alan Villiers	**Captain Cook**

READ MORE IN PENGUIN

PENGUIN CLASSIC HISTORY

Well written narrative history from leading historians such as Paul Kennedy, Alan Moorehead, J. B. Priestley, A. L. Rowse and G. M. Trevelyan. From the Ancient World to the decline of British naval mastery, from twelfth-century France to the Victorian Underworld, the series captures the great turning points in history and chronicles the lives of ordinary people at different times. Penguin Classic History will be enjoyed and valued by everyone who loves the past.

Published or forthcoming:

Leslie Alcock	**Arthur's Britain**
John Belchem/Richard Price	**A Dictionary of 19th-Century History**
Jeremy Black/Roy Porter	**A Dictionary of 18th-Century History**
Ernle Bradford	**The Mediterranean**
Anthony Burton	**Remains of a Revolution**
Robert Darnton	**The Great Cat Massacre**
Jean Froissart	**Froissart's Chronicles**
Johan Huizinga	**The Waning of the Middle Ages**
Aldous Huxley	**The Devils of Loudun**
Paul M. Kennedy	**The Rise and Fall of British Naval Mastery**
Margaret Wade Labarge	**Women in Medieval Life**
Alan Moorehead	**Fatal Impact**
Samuel Pepys	**Illustrated Pepys**
J. H. Plumb	**The First Four Georges**
J. B. Priestley	**The Edwardians**
Philippa Pullar	**Consuming Passions**
A. L. Rowse	**The Elizabethan Renaissance**
John Ruskin	**The Stones of Venice**
G. M. Trevelyan	**English Social History**
Philip Warner	**The Medieval Castle**
T. H. White	**The Age of Scandal**
Lawrence Wright	**Clean and Decent**
Hans Zinsser	**Rats, Lice and History**

READ MORE IN PENGUIN

PENGUIN CLASSIC MILITARY HISTORY

This series acknowledges the profound and enduring interest in military history, and the causes and consequences of human conflict. Penguin Classic Military History covers warfare from the earliest times to the age of electronics and encompasses subjects as diverse as classic examples of grand strategy and the precision tactics of Britain's crack SAS Regiment. The series will be enjoyed and valued by students of military history and all who hope to learn from the often disturbing lessons of the past.

Published or forthcoming:

Correlli Barnett	**Engage the Enemy More Closely**
	The Great War
David G. Chandler	**The Art of Warfare on Land**
	Marlborough as Military Commander
William Craig	**Enemy at the Gates**
Carlo D'Este	**Decision in Normandy**
Michael Glover	**The Peninsular War**
	Wellington as Military Commander
Winston Graham	**The Spanish Armadas**
Heinz Guderian	**Panzer Leader**
Christopher Hibbert	**Redcoats and Rebels**
Heinz Höhne	**The Order of the Death's Head**
Anthony Kemp	**The SAS at War**
Ronald Lewin	**Ultra Goes to War**
Martin Middlebrook	**The Falklands War**
	The First Day on the Somme
	The Kaiser's Battle
Desmond Seward	**Henry V**
John Toland	**Infamy**
Philip Warner	**Sieges of the Middle Ages**
Leon Wolff	**In Flanders Fields**
Cecil Woodham-Smith	**The Reason Why**